Colin Jackson
March 1991
8.4

Politics and the Christian Vision

POLITICS AND THE CHRISTIAN VISION

Paul Rowntree Clifford

SCM PRESS LTD

Clifford, Paul Rowntree
Politics and the Christian vision.
1. Christianity and politics
I. Title
261.7 BR115.P7

ISBN 0-334-02257-6

334 02257 6

First published 1984
by SCM Press Ltd
26–30 Tottenham Road, London N1 4BZ

Photoset at The Spartan Press Ltd
Lymington, Hants
and printed in Great Britain by
Richard Clay (The Chaucer Press) Ltd
Bungay, Suffolk

CONTENTS

INTRODUCTION

The impetus for this book arose out of explorations into setting up a Foundation for the Study of Christianity and Society which I was asked to undertake four years ago by the executive committee of the British Council of Churches. This led to several working parties and the establishment of a Forum of up to twenty people, with significant experience in different phases of public life and drawn from all the major Christian traditions, to investigate the contribution which Christians could make to the future shaping of British socicty.

That has inevitably raised the basic question of the value assumptions implied in the ordering of our public life. When these are uncovered, disillusionment, if not confusion, is found to prevail. Bishop Lesslie Newbigin, who has played a leading part in the inauguration of the Foundation, has argued in an important publication[1] that we have come to the end of an era marked by the predominance of a closed scientific world view stemming from the movement known as the 'Enlightenment' in the eighteenth century. From this perspective man has displaced God at the centre of the universe and science has been credited with the key to unlocking the secrets not only of nature but also of human society. All that, according to Newbigin, is now open to question. Despite the remarkable scientific and technological achievements of recent years, for which we should be profoundly grateful, the promise of a brave new world has not been realized. On the contrary, there is abundant evidence of the disintegration of Western society, and those whose hope rested on a Marxist panacea for all evils are being increasingly disillusioned by experience under Communist rule. Over the whole of our vaunted civilization lies the threat of a nuclear holocaust: the nemesis of the dream of the Enlightenment.

This fundamental questioning of the values governing modern society does not only come from Christian sources. For example, Professor Alasdair MacIntyre has recently argued that since the dawn of the Enlightenment moral values have become increasingly incoherent, with the consequence that Western society is left without any agreed standards on the basis of which it can be ordered.[2] He looks to a recovery of the classical virtues embodied in the Aristotelian-Christian tradition for the emergence of communities which can hold the door open to a more promising future. What cannot be reasonably challenged is that the value assumptions underlying the conduct of our political, economic and social affairs call for a fresh appraisal, and in this Christians have an important part to play.

The following pages are concerned with the Christian justification for and method of engagement in political affairs. This has recently become a matter of acute public controversy and in Chapter 1 I present the case for such involvement. In this I have interpreted politics in the widest sense to cover not only the legislative and administrative matters which are the business of the political parties and civil servants at all levels, but also every aspect of an individual's engagement in public life. I do not believe that a Christian analysis can properly separate the two because sometimes the realistic course of action is to press for legislative or structural change and sometimes to seek change from within the structures by the way in which a Christian works out his vocation. An example of this complementary approach is outlined in Chapter 6, 'Education for Living'.

The thesis developed in the opening chapter is that, when Christian values are at stake, we cannot rest content with enunciating general principles. Their relevance turns on the way in which they are cashed in terms of specific policies and programmes. That means reckoning with the provisional character of political theology, willingness to become involved in controversy and readiness to admit that we may be mistaken in our judgments. Central to my thesis is the conviction that the proper task for theology is to wrestle with the relativity of what can be achieved as we seek to be obedient to the heavenly vision in the transitory life of our pilgrimage on earth. That means forswearing all absolutes other than the givenness of the divine revelation in Jesus Christ our Lord. The application of that revelation to the ordering of human society must in the nature of the case be provisional and open to debate. Christians, therefore, are not entitled to claim that their political judgments are beyond question or are to be unambiguously identified with the will of God, but that does not absolve them from making the best judgments they can in the light of the faith they profess, always being open to correction and fresh insights.

Accordingly, from Chapter 2 onwards I have ventured to suggest a way of approaching the main political questions of the day from an avowedly Christian standpoint. Of course, this does not mean dealing with detailed questions of policy. That would be a fruitless exercise, even if it were possible, because specific legislation and administrative decisions are in response to changing situations which have to be faced in the light of what is practicable at the time. Although I believe that value assumptions ultimately lie behind every decision and that this is how they are seen to be cashed, the important thing is to identify the broad approach to policies in the light of which the more detailed decisions are taken. If this is held to be settling for what have been called 'middle axioms' – broad lines of policy as distinct from general principles – I still hold to the view adopted in the opening chapter that it is the way in which these are cashed in practice that ultimately defines them.

Adopting a Christian frame of reference for political judgment is to enter a minefield. When unpalatable conclusions are reached, the accusation is likely to be made that the secular premises of political opponents lie behind what is advocated. That was the essence of the charge of leftward tendencies levelled against church leaders by Dr Edward Norman in his Reith Lectures[3] and more recently advanced by the authors of the symposium *The Kindness That Kills*,[4] though they are manifestly open to the same charge in reverse. The danger is always present of buttressing political predilections and prejudices by selective appeals to the Bible and the Christian tradition rather than subjecting them to a rigorous theological critique. Difficult as it may be, it is essential to preserve the Christian perspective, conducting the debate on those premises and no other.

Much of what I have to say, especially in the later chapters, is highly controversial, and I claim to speak for no one but myself. While I have greatly benefitted from the discussions which have taken place under the auspices of the Foundation for the Study of Christianity and Society, nobody else is represented by the views I have expressed. From the beginning it has been the hope of all concerned that the studies initiated would stimulate participants to write books and articles on their own responsibility, and this is one of them.

Bishop Lesslie Newbigin has been kind enough to read the whole typescript and has made a number of valuable suggestions which I have tried to take into account. My gratitude is also due to Mr and Mrs Duncan McNeil of Kippford who have painstakingly and accurately transcribed my erratic handwriting and prepared the typescript for publication.

April 1984 Paul Rowntree Clifford
Dalbeattie, Scotland

I

Why Politics?

Most British people are confused about politics. Underlying this is a deeper confusion about the kind of society we want to have and the values which should inform it. Those on the right and left who confidently proclaim that they have the answers are increasingly viewed with scepticism, and for evidence of this we need to look no further than the fluctuations in the opinion polls. Only a small minority of the population are paid-up members of any political party, while many of those who confine themselves to voting at elections – and they are less than half entitled to do so for local authorities – are motivated by habit rather than by any strong convictions. Many others do not bother to vote at all, believing that it makes very little difference to them which candidates get elected. Politics is all too commonly regarded as a power game played by those who are principally concerned with securing office. This was encapsulated some years ago in the lines which brought down the curtain at a play on Broadway entitled *The State of the Union*. 'What's the difference between a Republican and a Democrat?' 'All the difference in the world,' was the reply. 'They're in and we're out!'

Nevertheless, politics is about the way in which society is structured: the context within which ordinary people have to live out their daily lives. While that obviously affects everyone, nowadays many feel that the issues are too complex for them to understand. What happens at Westminster or even on the local council appears remote from their everyday concerns about holding down a job, managing a family, meeting with friends, pursuing hobbies, sharing the companionship of club, pub, society or church. That is why so many say 'I'm not political' or 'I'm not interested in politics.'

This betrays an underlying confusion about the meaning of the word. Politics literally means 'the things concerning the city': that is to say, the way in which we are related to one another through conventions, rules, laws and institutions. In other words, it is the structuring of human relations. In this broad sense all the activities referred to above are political; for they are concerned with human relationships. Only a hermit is, strictly speaking, non-political. That is where we have to start rethinking our politics; for we have been misled into supposing that a person is to be defined as an isolated individual who can pursue his or her own private affairs without regard to anyone else. That is to deal in an abstraction. Human beings are what they are in relation to one another. Babies are dependent on their mothers from birth and grow up in an expanding network of relationships which mould the shaping of character from day to day. Left alone, the baby would die. Isolated from all human contact an adult would disintegrate.

Therefore, we are bound to be concerned about the structure of human relationships and the values which inform them. This applies to what most people would regard as the basic unit of the family and extends to the whole network of relationships in the local community and beyond to the nation and world at large. As we begin to question the way in which we live together in our several neighbourhoods, we shall begin to see the relevance of what we normally refer to as politics: the ordering of our corporate life as a nation; the extension of the family into the body politic. How ordinary people can best make a contribution to the total political process will occupy us in the next chapter on 'Democracy and Participation'. Here it is sufficient to establish the point that politics is the proper concern of everyone. To pretend that you can contract out is to resort to untenable individualism. We are essentially political beings.

Of course, this invites the objection that politics is being defined in a far too wide and misleading sense. We ought to restrict it to the institutional structures of the state and not extend it to community associations or voluntary organizations. Nothing but confusion results from lumping everything together. Admittedly, a distinction has to be drawn between those institutions which order public life as a whole and those concerned with sectional interests. But if too sharp a distinction is made, the fact that politics in the commonly understood sense is about human relations is likely to be obscured. In all that follows I shall be principally concerned with the public sphere and the institutions of government. However, the discussion gets off on the wrong foot unless the underlying assumptions are brought out into the open. The wider context of human relations is the only acceptable framework within which specific political problems can realistically be tackled. To deny that is to cut the ground from understanding what our responsibilities are and leads to a disastrous divorce between public and private life.

In all this, values are at stake. What kind of a society do we want to see emerging from the confusion of our times? On what principles should our common life be ordered? How far are popular aspirations and attitudes responsible for social disintegration? Is the disillusionment with politicians and political parties based on confusion about the values which should inform their policies or even on false values which for one reason or another have come to be widely adopted?

Christians cannot escape these questions; for they have to do with God's purpose for his creation. Nevertheless, it is probably true that a significant proportion of British Christians do not believe that the church should be involved in politics, or at least are confused about what that involvement should be. As for the public at large, the general view seems to be that religion is the private affair of those so inclined, of little or no social importance.

This rejection of any tenable connexion between Christianity and politics has recently been expressed in its most extreme form by Enoch Powell. Reviewing a book on the subject by the Chaplain of an Oxford college, he dismisses it as 'a brave try' because he believes that 'the Gospel has three fundamental characteristics which defeat any "Christian approach to politics": it is pacifist; it is eschatological; and it is individualistic'.[1] The simplistic way in which Enoch Powell interprets these three words does scant justice to the far more complex teaching of the Bible.

Later in his review he defines pacifism as passivity: an identification which no Christian pacifist would be likely to accept and which certainly is a caricature of Jesus himself. The gospels do not present him as someone who meekly accepted everything people said or did to him. His whole ministry was an attack on evil wherever it was to be found and his death and resurrection were seen by his followers as a conquest of the powers dominating the world. How the resistance of Jesus and his teaching about loving our enemies is to be applied to the modern world under the threat of a nuclear holocaust is a matter of serious debate amongst Christians. It cannot be dismissed in cavalier fashion as mere passivity having no relevance to our contemporary struggles.

However, the real force of Enoch Powell's case is centred on his belief that Jesus was simply concerned with individuals in their isolation and with eschatology understood as what lies beyond the life of the individual on earth and the end of history. The fatal flaw in this interpretation is that it picks out a strand in the teaching of Jesus and the Bible as a whole and then, without regard to the total context, elevates it to become the entire content of the gospel. For a start, it entails discarding virtually the whole of the Old Testament, concerned as it is with the emergence of Israel as a nation, the ordering of her life under a succession of leaders and the working out of her relationship with neighbouring peoples and the surrounding empires. The Ten Commandments were the foundation of Israel's social structure, and detailed regulations, such as we find in the Book of Leviticus, were promulgated to cover every aspect of the people's relations with one another, with strangers within their gates and with the tribes inhabiting the adjoining regions. Later, the prophets exercised the role of guardians of the nation's standards, condemning corruption within and false alliances without. Over the whole field of domestic and foreign relationships the will of God was held to be supreme. It was believed to be his purpose to make Israel a nation ordered according to his law of righteousness and thereby a light to all the nations on earth. The concept of a secular state, governed according to the wishes of its members but allowing room for individual religious practice, is about as foreign as anything could be to the beliefs of the leaders and prophets of Israel. They were concerned with applying the will of God as they understood it to the nation as a corporate entity; the rights and duties of individuals could be understood only within that context.

With the arrival of Jesus on the scene, there was admittedly a radical change of emphasis, but not so radical as to constitute a complete break in continuity with the past. Certainly he turned his back on any notion of what might be called a theocratic state playing power politics and challenging the might of the now supreme Roman Empire. He saw the futility of all pretensions to raise the standard of revolt, and he grieved over the city of Jerusalem, the destruction of which he foretold if the machinations of the various factions at work were allowed to continue. On the contrary he proclaimed the advent of a new kingdom, the reign which God had inaugurated in his own coming and which would stand in judgment upon the disintegration and collapse of all humanly devised political orders.

The kingdom of God is central to the teaching of Jesus, interpreted by St Paul as the reconciliation of all people and all things in Christ.[2] That is not to be reduced simply to the salvation of individuals; their reconciliation to God brings them into organic relation with one another.[3] Nor is this just to be postponed to life after death or the end of history. New Testament scholars have long recognized that there is an element of 'realized eschatology' in the teaching of Jesus and the testimony of the apostolic church. The consummation of the kingdom undoubtedly lies beyond the world's history, but it has already been decisively inaugurated in the advent of Jesus; or, to put it another way, the future consummation impinges upon the here and now, challenging all human pretensions to construct a social order that rests on finite interests and ambitions. Since the coming of Christ we are, according to St Paul, those upon whom 'the fulfilment of the ages has come' or, more graphically translated, 'those who live in the overlap of the ages'.[4]

Enoch Powell is just wrong. Whatever the difficulty of relating the Bible to the complexities of the modern world – and the difficulty is considerable – a careful study of the scriptures and the New Testament in particular does not substantiate any of the three propositions he holds to be self-evident. The teaching of Jesus does not enjoin sheer passivity; it is not exclusively confined to an extra-terrestrial kingdom; and it is not addressed to the individual in his isolation. Religion does have to do with a person in his uniqueness, in the individuality of his relationship to God in faith and prayer, but the whole person is involved, and, that, by definition, includes his inter-relationship with other people. Individuality is a fact, but it has to be understood in relational terms.

That is why the church is an inescapable corollary of the gospel. It is not merely a voluntary association of like-minded people similar to a society for bee-keeping or stamp collecting. Even if it were just that, it would be concerned with structural relationships. But its essence can only properly be evaluated in organic terms; those who are related to God through baptism, faith and commitment belong to one another. This was expounded by St Paul in his analogy of the body in I Corinthians 12: 'A body is not one single organ, but many. Suppose the foot should say, "Because I am not a hand, I do not belong to the body' it does belong to the body none the less. Suppose the ear were to say, "Because I am not an eye, I do not belong to the body," it does still belong to the body. If the body were all eye, how could it hear? If the body were all ear, how could it smell? But, in fact, God appointed each limb and organ to its own place in the body, as he chose. If one organ suffers, they all suffer together. If one flourishes, they all rejoice together. Now you are Christ's body, and each of you a limb or organ of it.'[5] In so far, then, as we understand politics in its widest sense as having to do with the structure of human relationships, the church is itself a political entity.

Doubtless that will come as a startling assertion to those who are accustomed to regard attendance at church as one activity alongside many others engaging them during the week and having limited relevance to what they do every day. The church then becomes a clerical institution providing what are sometimes called the 'rites of passage' – baptism, marriage and burial – and offering spiritual aids to those inclined to seek them. On this view it differs very little in principle from a medical centre or the corner shop except that it is less commonly used. But those who are prepared to take the Christian gospel seriously are bound to see this as a caricature of what the church is meant to be. It is charged with proclaiming the good news of the reconciliation of men, women and children to God, uniting them to one another through faith in him and commissioning them as a corporate body to be heralds of his kingdom: a pattern for the community at large of what God intends it to be. The fact that the church so often fails to make this plain because of the frailty of its members and their own misunderstanding of their vocation does not affect the purpose of God or alter the inner meaning of the gospel. St Paul's analogy of the body of Christ is an essential expression of the Christian faith.

But those who are members of the Christian church are also members of society at large. If acceptance of the gospel has brought them into relationship with one another, it also has implications for their relationship with other people. This is not the same as sharing a common faith, but it does provide the touchstone for the values which they are led to believe should govern the structures of society as a whole. Therefore, the assumption that Christianity has nothing to do with politics because it is solely concerned with an individual's relationship to God is fundamentally mistaken.

The immediate objection to this line of argument is likely to be an appeal to the reply Jesus gave to the Pharisees and Herodians when they asked him whether taxes should be paid to Caesar or not. It is held that when he told them, 'Render unto Caesar the things that are Caesar's and to God the things that are God's',[6] he was enunciating the principle of two distinct spheres of responsibility: the secular government and the spiritual domain. Whenever the assertion is made that the church should not interfere in politics, with the concession that it has its own proper sphere of influence which the secular power should not attempt to control, this saying of Jesus is almost invariably quoted, with St Paul's injunctions in his letter to the Romans cited in support: 'Let every person be subject to the governing authorities. For there is no authority except from God. Therefore he who resists the authorities resists what God appointed, and those who resist will incur judgment. . . . Pay all of them their dues, taxes to whom taxes are due, revenue to whom revenue is due, respect to whom respect is due, honour to whom honour is due.'[7] This was undoubtedly the foundation on which the church of the first four centuries sought to come to terms with the Roman empire. It was made quite explicit in a letter Hosius of Cordova addressed to the emperor Constantius at a time of acute theological controversy into which he sought to intervene: 'Intrude not yourself into ecclesiastical matters, neither give commands unto us concerning them; but learn them from us. God has put into your hands the kingdom; to us he has entrusted the affairs of his church; and as he who would steal the empire from you would resist the ordinance of God, so likewise fear on your part lest by taking upon yourself the government of the Church, you become guilty of a great offence. It is written, "Render unto Caesar the things that are Caesar's and unto God the things that are God's." Neither therefore is it permitted unto us to exercise earthly rule, nor have you, Sire, any authority to burn incense.'[8]

But can these texts bear the weight that has been placed upon them? Peter Hinchliff in the book reviewed by Enoch Powell argues that they cannot; the conclusion drawn from a superficial reading misses the whole point. The question Jesus asked was, 'Whose image and superscription is this?' 'Caesar's,' was the reply. Because it bore Caesar's image, it could properly be given to Caesar, but whose image does man bear? The answer is God's. Therefore *you* belong to God: the whole of man being in God's image. Accordingly all human life, including the political sphere, belongs to God.[9]

This is indeed to cut the Gordian knot. Personally, I find the exegesis over-subtle and unconvincing. It seems to me to be much more plausible to treat the saying as a trick answer to a trick question. Jesus was confronted with an attempt on the part of Pharisees and Herodians together to trap him into saying something which could be used either as evidence of treason or else as a means of discrediting him in the eyes of the people: should the Jews pay tribute to Caesar or not? Turning the tables on his questioners, Jesus replied in deliberately enigmatic terms, avoiding any definition of the realm of Caesar or the realm of God, even leaving undecided whether the two realms could be separated. On another occasion he had done very much the same thing. Asked by the chief priests, the scribes and the elders wherein lay the authority for his actions, Jesus countered with a question about the nature of John's baptism.[10] If he had given a direct reply his words would have been misinterpreted and used against him; so he placed his opponents in the same position. Both incidents are examples of the skill with which Jesus could handle a difficult situation and outwit those who tried to ensnare him. Neither provides us with definitive principles on which we should venture to construct a body of doctrine.

Whichever interpretation is correct, the fact of the matter is that an enormous theoretical edifice has been erected on the most insubstantial foundation. When Jesus spoke about rendering to Caesar the things that are Caesar's and to God the things that are God's, it is very doubtful whether he was enunciating a general principle at all; certainly it cannot be taken for granted and used as the major premise for Christian sociological teaching. As for Romans 13, no other option was open to Paul. The Roman empire provided the framework of peace and order within which the early church could carry out its mission. As long as that situation prevailed, there was no reason to challenge the secular authority; it was fulfilling a divine ordinance. But when persecution began, the situation radically changed; the two spheres could no longer be kept apart, and throughout the succeeding centuries the clear-cut and superficially easy solution to the problem of church-state relations has proved to be unrealistic, only made possible by the privatizing of religion which has been one of the unfortunate legacies of the Enlightenment.

Certainly there is a distinction between the two spheres, and whenever church and state have been identified, as with the mediæval papacy or Calvin's short-lived experiment in Geneva to establish a theocratic regime, the church's proper role has been hopelessly compromised. Dante's condemnation of the papacy in his own day stands as a classical warning of what can happen when the proper distinction is forgotten: 'Rome, that made the good world, was wont to have two suns, which made plain to sight the one road and the other; that of the world and that of God. One hath quenched the other, and the sword is joined to the crook; and the one together with the other must perforce go ill, because, being joined, one feareth not the other.'[11]

The quotation from Dante suggests the proper relation between church and state: tension rather than separation: the tension between witness to the eternal verities and responsibility for ordering temporal affairs. This was the theme of St Augustine's great treatise in the fifth century which he called *The City of God*. Following the fall of Rome to Alaric and his barbarian hordes, the cry was raised that the calamity was due to the forsaking of the ancient gods upon whom the protection of the city and empire had always depended; the adoption of Christianity after the accession of Constantine had been an unmitigated disaster for Rome. Such was the pagan argument which Augustine set himself to answer.

He describes his purpose as the defence of 'the glorious City of God against those who prefer their own gods to its Founder', contrasting it with the earthly city 'which lusts to dominate the world and which, though nations bend to its yoke, is itself dominated by its passion for dominion'.[12] Throughout the whole of the twenty-two books Augustine makes it plain that he does not regard the earthly city, organized by man for his own ends, as having any enduring value. In fact, strictly speaking, it is not a city at all. For if Cicero is right in claiming that the state can only properly be described as existing when it is founded on justice,[13] this has never been the case in pagan society, because justice is only possible when the true God is given his due; and that only happens in the city of God.[14]

The title of his work really summarizes the position which Augustine adopts: he does not call it 'The Two Cities', because the earthly city only interests him by contrast with the city of God, the community of the faithful, which endures to eternity and alone gives life on earth any meaning. He even goes so far as to discount the significance of different forms of government: 'When it is considered,' he writes, 'how short is the span of human life, does it really matter to a man whose days are numbered what government he must obey, so long as he is not compelled to act against God or his conscience?'[15] True, under earthly conditions, the history of the two cities is inextricably intermingled,[16] but it is only the city of God that has positive value. At best the earthly city is a necessary evil, and the peace it establishes provisional. 'The heavenly city, meanwhile – or, rather, that part that is on pilgrimage in mortal life and lives by faith – must use this earthly peace until such time as our mortality which needs such peace has passed away.'[17] The earthly city is founded to counter man's sin,[18] and is thus negative in purpose. No lasting happiness is to be found in it;[19] though the Christian who is subject to earthly rulers may enjoy such happiness even in his subjection because of his citizenship in the city of God.[20]

The broad conclusion of Augustine's argument would therefore appear to be other-worldly in character: the earthly city and its organization is of no lasting importance: Christians should be concerned with that eternal city whose builder and maker is God. Yet the matter is not quite so simple. Augustine would have believers take their civic responsibilities seriously, and even argues that the salvation of the Roman Empire ultimately turns on the Christian virtue of its citizens. In a letter to Marcellinus he replies to those who say that the teaching of Christ is opposed to the welfare of the state by bidding them 'produce such provincial administrators, such husbands, such wives, such parents, such sons, such masters, such slaves, such kings, such judges, and finally such tax-payers and collectors of public revenue as Christian teaching requires them to be, and then let them dare to say that this teaching is opposed to the welfare of the state, or, rather, let them even hesitate to admit that it is the greatest safety of the state, if it is observed.'[21] The earthly city could approximate to the shadow of the heavenly city, but in the last resort it is provisional and therefore must never be absolutized.

Augustine stated the problem of church-state relations rather than solved it, and it proved all too easy for those who came afterwards to get rid of the tension either by identifying church and state or by developing the doctrine of the two spheres, as Luther did, enjoining a strict separation between them. It has frequently been pointed out that many of the troubles in Europe over the past four hundred years are traceable to the baneful effect of Luther's teaching on the relationship of church and state; for where it has been predominant, it has resulted in the abdication of Christian witness from any leadership in the field of social and international affairs. The state has been allowed to go to the devil if it would, because in the nature of the case the church had no guidance to give, no rightful influence to exert. Thus in the 1930s Nazism came to power in Germany in the moral and political vacuum for which other-worldly privatized religion was in no small measure accountable. On the other hand, we must not forget that when the totalitarianism of the Hitler regime became apparent and the so-called German Christians became a tool in the hands of the Nazi leadership, the confessional movement came to birth within the Lutheran Church leading to the now famous

Barmen declaration, echoing the words of the apostle, 'We ought to obey God rather than men.'[22] Any attempt to minimize or avoid the tension will not do. Since the members of the church are also citizens of the state and the state is itself held to be a divine ordinance no strict separation between the two spheres is defensible. The values of the kingdom of God will always be in tension with the practice of politics, though we should look for that tension to be as creative as possible.

How is that to be achieved? For the past fifty years or so the approach most commonly adopted has been to derive guiding principles from the Bible for the ordering of public affairs. The dominating figure behind this in Britain was William Temple, who as the outstanding spokesman of the established church in the 1920s and 1930s used his considerable influence to challenge both church and nation to face the social implications of the gospel. He maintained that there are certain abiding principles, unaffected by the passage of time, which have nevertheless to be applied to changing social circumstances, their working out in terms of practical policies depending on the special knowledge and expertise of those engaged in public administration and in the direction of economic and industrial affairs. It is the task of the church, Temple contended, to enunciate these principles as the God-given standard in the light of which all practical programmes and policies are to be judged, calling on people of good will everywhere to accept them as the basis for social reconstruction.

Temple formulated these overriding principles derived from the gospel as freedom, social fellowship and service, though, as Ronald Preston points out in his commemorative article on the occasion of the centenary of Temple's birth, 'it is surprising that he did not extend his trilogy to include equality, particularly in view of his close association with R. H. Tawney for whom this was crucial'.[23] Others might wish to add to his derivative principles love, justice, mutual responsibility and reconciliation, though Temple would probably have argued that these are subsumed under his three headings when they have been adequately spelt out and expanded. At all events, his three derivative principles provided the foundation for the influential COPEC conference in Birmingham in 1924, which was followed by public meetings addressed by Temple himself, and his widely read Penguin book,

Christianity and the Social Order,[24] leading up to the Oxford conference on Church, Community and State in 1937, in which Temple played a prominent part.

The COPEC and Oxford conferences, for which a great deal of special expertise was marshalled, both produced impressive and extensive reports which still repay careful study. In spite of the intervention of the Second World War, which brought the momemtum of the discussion to a halt, and Temple's untimely death in 1944, the influence of this whole movement of the 1920s and 1930s, if that is what it can be called, has continued to be felt, even though it has waned. Many of those charged with responding in the name of the churches to the challenge of contemporary society appear to be drawing on the capital of the Temple period in default of any clear conviction about a different way of tackling today's problems. At the same time there is a growing consensus that Temple's approach, important as it was in the inter-war years in awakening the churches from their inward-looking ecclesiastical preoccupations and alerting Christians to their public responsibilities, is no longer adequate as a response to the contemporary situation.

There are several reasons for saying this. In the first place, the context is very different. Temple's influence was exercised at a time when the British Empire still covered a large part of the surface of the globe and at its heart was a nation which, in spite of widespread alienation from the churches, was still held together by the sort of values to which Temple could appeal in enunciating his three derivative principles. Moreover, the problems of the 1930s – the rise of totalitarianism on the continent of Europe and the hardship and poverty resulting from the economic depression at home – all appeared to be capable of being overcome given sufficient resolution and commitment to the principles which Temple was upholding. In other words, the leader of the Anglican Church could speak out as the conscience of the nation and expect to be listened to with respect both at home and abroad.

All that has changed. Britain has lost her leading role in world affairs as new nations have come into being and the new superpowers have divided their spheres of influence in growing hostility to one another, threatening mutual destruction on a scale that no one could have envisaged in the pre-war period. The rapid growth of multi-national corporations and the ramifications of international finance have severely curtailed the ability of any one country to control its economy, and at the same time we have become aware of the danger to future generations from the exploitation of the natural environment, leading to the depletion of scarce resources and the pollution of the seas, the rivers, the land and the atmosphere. In the face of all this ordinary people have come to feel helpless, and the temptation to retreat into a privatized life has become overwhelming. Any appeal to a social conscience is much more problematic now than when Temple was alive. On the home front Britain has become a multi-racial, pluralist society which has not found its cohesion in any set of values claiming the allegiance of the population at large. Indeed, there are ominous signs of disintegration not only in the polarization of political parties, conflict in industry, racial tension and bitter division between the ghettos of deprivation and the rest of the population, but also in the growing number of people for whom self-interest at any cost to others has become a way of life. We should not underrate the significance of the rise in the crime rate, particularly as it is only the tip of the iceberg. These are some of the features of the contemporary scene.

In the second place, implicit in this change of context is the sense that the problems we face today are far more complex and intractable and far less susceptible to Christian influence than those with which the pre-war generation had to deal. The seeds of this perplexity were somewhat surprisingly sown in the United States, where confident optimism about the possibility of overcoming any problem so long prevailed. It was the home of liberal Protestantism where under the influence of Walter Rauschenbuch and others the so-called social gospel held sway, promising steady progress towards the establishment of the kingdom of God. It matched the American dream that nothing was beyond the power of human achievement, a dream only finally shattered by the war in Vietnam.

But against this unlikely background a prophetic voice was raised in the person of Reinhold Niebuhr, who subjected the optimistic liberal Protestantism of his day to devastating criticism and whose influence was felt far beyond the borders of the United States. In a series of publications spread over a lifetime, Niebuhr set himself to challenge what he saw as the simplistic application of the law of love to the economic, social and political problems faced by the industralized Western nations. This, he held, failed to take at all seriously the stubborn factor of human sin, and he proceeded to a radical analysis of man's condition, exposing any naive optimism about the perfectablility of society. Central to his thesis was the conviction that group behaviour is always and inevitably on a lower moral level than that of individuals, and this makes the intractability of social, economic and political problems that much greater. Politics, therefore, is the sphere of the relative, and Christians have the duty to face this dilemma, not expecting that there are any ideal solutions, but prepared to strive for the best that can be done in the light of the faith that they profess.

No one can deny the penetrating quality of Niebuhr's analysis nor overestimate the service he rendered in compelling his contemporaries to face with stark realism the kind of world in which they were living. All his writings are like a douche of cold water upon the sloppy sentimentalism and shallow wishful thinking which characterized so many expectations in the inter-war years. Indeed, his influence continues to be felt, the penetration of his analysis of the human condition and the realism of his political outlook probably having much more lasting impact on Christian social thinking than that of his great contemporary, William Temple.

In the third place, the context has changed in that its focus has dramatically shifted from Britain, and indeed from the Western nations, to other parts of the world. Even if this has not been fully recognized as yet by people in general, Christians have every reason to know that it is so. The change in the composition of the World Council of Churches, where the voice of the nations of Africa, Asia and Latin America has become increasingly predominant, is sufficient evidence of a far-reaching alteration in the focus of Christian concern. Temple's derivative principles, though undoubtedly reflecting features of the gospel, have a distinctively British middle-class ring about them. It is perhaps not too unfair to say that one hears the public-spirited ex-headmaster of Repton speaking. That is not to devalue the genuine Christian conviction underlying everything Temple stood for, but it contrasts sharply with the liberation theology which has been emanating from Latin

America over the past few years and is increasingly echoed in the voices of Asians and Africans. For them the main theme of the biblical story is God's identification with the poor and the oppressed, rooted in the Exodus of the Hebrew slaves from Egypt and confirmed in the announcement of his mission by Jesus in the synagogue at Nazareth 'to preach the gospel to the poor . . . to heal the broken-hearted, to preach deliverance to the captives, and recovering of sight to the blind, to set at liberty them that are bruised, to preach the acceptable year of the Lord'.[25] Throughout his ministry Jesus sided with the outcasts and underprivileged of society against the political and religious establishments of the day. This is the charter for collaboration with any who are similarly committed to the deliverance of the oppressed, whether they be Marxists or humanists.

Christians in the West have not yet fully come to terms with this radical change of emphasis. There has been a growing recognition that it is an authentic expression of the gospel which has a great deal to say to those of us who live in relative affluence, not least when we face up to the areas of poverty and deprivation at the heart of our great cities. Moreover, the exponents of liberation theology are not simply talking about identification with the oppressed; they are doing something about it, struggling with and alongside those who are the victims of monstrous injustice, often at the cost of their liberty and even their lives. It has been a hard lesson to learn for many Christians in Europe and North America, long accustomed to think of the church as a bastion of established authority. The widespread unease amongst ordinary people in the pew about the World Council of Churches' special fund to combat racism and grants such as that made to the Toxteth Residents Defence Association following riots on the streets of Liverpool are evidence enough of that.

But when full recognition has been given to the struggle for liberation and a place in the sun for all who are exploited and oppressed as a valid, and indeed inescapable mandate of the gospel, the question remains unanswered how we are to work out its implications in our own context of affluence. Quite apart from this, we are left wondering what are the guidelines for any society where the mighty have actually been cast down from their seats. There is the danger that one tyranny will replace another; and the experience of Marxist regimes, for example, allegedly based on the overthrow of capitalist exploitation to give power to the people, does not encourage anyone to believe that the fight for liberation will of itself produce a more humane society. The exponents of Latin American theology recognize this as clearly as anyone else and are seeking to find a constructive way forward within their own highly problematic context. We must strive to do the same in our own, but it is a very different context from that in which Temple operated. It is now determined by a world in transition and turmoil to a degree that those of previous generations could scarcely have envisaged.

Thus far I have been speaking of the radical change in context within which we have to do our theology from that in which William Temple exercised such commanding influence. There is, however, a more fundamental issue at stake, implicit in what I have said about the impact of Reinhold Niebuhr and liberation theology. Is it any longer satisfactory to derive general principles from the gospel, regarding their enunciation as the distinctive Christian contribution to the resolution of our social, economic and political problems? The alarm signals should be set at red when the word 'theology' has come to be used in popular discourse for a theoretical argument which has no practical bearing on decisions that have to be taken in the real world. What do general principles mean unless they are cashed in terms of specific policies, programmes and actions? This is true even of such an assertion as 'God is love'. As Nathaniel Micklem once wrote, 'Only when we have said that God *so* loved, do we know what it means that God is Love, for this is not an abstract proposition in philosophy, but the adoring apprehension of a saving act.'[26] Temple would have had no difficulty in agreeing with that; for his theology was based on the doctrine of the Incarnation and he drew his inspiration for social ethics from that source. But at the same time there was a strong background of Platonism to his thinking with its emphasis on eternal ideas and absolute verities, which accorded with the widespread assumption that Christianity deals in absolutes, not in relativities. Therefore, a sharp distinction was possible between the unchanging principles derived from the gospel and the relativity of their incarnation in social, economic and political policies.

One attempt to suggest a way of bridging the gap between Temple's general principles and the detailed political, economic and social policies which are admittedly a matter of controversy amongst those who conscientiously seek to bear witness to their Christian faith was the notion of 'middle axioms': a formula canvassed by J. H. Oldham at the Oxford conference in 1937. In the introductory volume written in collaboration with Dr Visser t'Hooft, these middle axioms are described as 'an attempt to define the directions in which, in a particular state of society, Christian faith must express itself. They are not binding for all time, but are provisional definitions of the type of behaviour of Christians in a given period and given circumstances.[27] An example might be: the government has the responsibility for maintaining full employment. This is a political judgment which goes a good deal further than the unexceptionable and much more general assertion that God is concerned with the welfare of all human beings, which no Christian would be likely to challenge.

Ronald Preston in a more recent paper on the subject maintains that this was a helpful development, to be taken seriously by those who are wrestling with the social ethics of today. Convinced that the enunciation of general principles is inadequate, he is afraid of any commitment to specific policies because they are dependent upon empirical data, the interpretation of which is open to question. To quote his own words, 'They are disputable because they involve a whole series of judgments about the facts of an issue, and the possible consequences of different lines of action, about which there are inescapable uncertainties (if only because we cannot foresee with certainty), and therefore more than one possible option.'[28]

This amounts to saying that we must not take the risk of being wrong, or, if we do that, we are stepping beyond the limits of a Christian application of the gospel to political affairs. But even the middle axiom itself may be open to challenge from a Christian perspective. In the case of the example I have taken there are undoubtedly those who would argue that a concern for the welfare of people requires the government to renounce responsibility for full employment because that will be achieved only by allowing market forces to operate freely. If middle axioms are controversial and open to challenge, why should we stop short at specific policies for translating them into practice?

Refusal to do so may well be a recipe for irrelevance. It is my conviction that principles have to be cashed in specific policies to see what they really mean; and that applies to middle axioms no less than more general statements. Middle axioms may be a useful stage on the way to clarifying policies, but if we stop there at a sort of half-way stage, we shall be like spectators of an affray in the streets from the upper floor windows who feel that they ought to be part of the action and come down the stairs as far as the landing only to decide to go no further.

In short, we have to take seriously the contention that principles are *defined* by their application and therefore, considered in themselves, they are mere abstractions or generalizations. Principles are never fixed or finalized, but develop in content when interpreted within changing contexts. If that is conceded, then the real theological task does not consist in theorizing, but in wrestling with the concrete problems that face us, acknowledging the relativity and controversial nature of any conclusions we may reach. Doing theology is not thinking divorced from practice, nor is it abandoning thinking in favour of action in the hope that theology will thereby be clarified. It is thinking about what we are actually doing or are preparing to do, and that entails analysing our commitments to specific policies.

Nevertheless, the proposal to bring Christian values to bear on the political, economic and social questions of the day is enough to set the alarm bells ringing in many quarters. Recent events in Iran, Northern Ireland and Israel, involving three of the world's great religions, seem to have provided conclusive testimony to the disastrous consequences of allowing religion to dominate politics. Moreover, they are not isolated examples. History has been bedevilled by religious wars, and the incursion of the institutional church into politics has so often led to intolerance, persecution and oppression. No wonder that many people would view with consternation any suggestion that religion has a part to play in the political process; any attempt to impose beliefs that stem from a particular tradition would be fiercely resisted by those who do not adhere to them. Given the history of the past and the all too familiar contemporary examples of sectarian bigotry, surely we should have nothing to do with any idea of introducing the claims of religion into the politial arena.

This is a perfectly understandable reaction. Religion has so often proved to be a seed bed for fanaticism and even where more moderate and balanced views have prevailed there has often been a tendency to claim absolute monopoly of the truth with resulting intolerance towards those who do not subscribe to a given version of it. There is a dangerous progression from holding that values are grounded in the purpose of God, to a claim to be the privileged interpreters of the divine will, to the insistence that this should be accepted by the rest of society. Fanatical intolerance and ruthless oppression of all dissident opinion are simply the extreme expression of this all too common religious claim. The Ayatolla Khomenei has appeared to carry only to its logical conclusion the conviction that the will of God should prevail in the ordering of society.

Wherever Islam is predominant and its adherents are instructed to believe that the Koran contains detailed laws for the regulation of human society, the climate is prepared for their enforcement; for anything else is contrary to the will of Allah. Similarly, orthodox Jews in the modern State of Israel have sought to use their political power to impose a strict observance of the Torah on what is a predominantly secular society. If the church were to try to put the clock back to mediaeval times and seek the prerogative to order human affairs, resistance to it would be overwhelming, and rightly so. But that is not what is being claimed. Any such pretension is foreclosed by the very nature of the God in whom Christians believe. He is revealed as having infinite patience, never imposing his will on mankind. What he does not do, Christians are not entitled to do in his name. Therefore, while they are commissioned to bear testimony to the purpose of God in so far as they are able to apprehend it and to insist that society is bound to disintegrate unless it is ordered according to values enshrined in the gospel – and there is plenty of evidence of this as we look at the mess we human beings have made of the world – there is no justification for any claim to domination. Perhaps this is one of the major contributions that Christians have to make in the face of growing political intolerance, exhibited in unwillingness to listen to a contrary point of view or even allow it to be expressed, threatening coups which override the will of minorities and majorities alike.

Deep convictions can be held without any recourse to domination; indeed the refusal to countenance all forms of dictatorship is central to a Christian understanding of the nature and purpose of God. That is the answer to those who for highly justifiable reasons fear the incursion of religion into politics.

A nagging question remains. I have argued that it is not sufficient for the church to enunciate general principles; they have a cutting edge only when they are cashed in terms of specific policies with all the relativity and ambiguity which that entails. But there are those who believe that this compromises the church's proper role. It should stand above the party debate and stick to general principles, leaving their working out to those actually engaged in the political arena. This is the major thesis of a recent book by the sociologist, Robin Gill.[29] He maintains that failure to make the distinction is to confuse prophecy with priesthood. The latter is the function of the church, ministering to all sorts and conditions of people, of all political persuasions and none. Prophecy, or the application of the gospel to social, political and economic affairs, is essentially sectarian; it can only properly be undertaken by those with particular convictions who speak for themselves and not for the church as a whole. To demand, therefore, that the church should give a lead on public questions is to divide it and make it ineffective in fulfilling its proper task. Prophets are needed who will stick out their necks, but they should not pretend that they can speak on behalf of all Christians. If the church, or more accurately the churches, keep to general principles, they may be criticized for vagueness, but they may still perform an invaluable service in defending those values which Gill holds to be deeply embedded in our national consciousness and which are now subject to attack or may easily be discarded in the advance of a secular age.

This is a persuasive argument, but it seems to me to rest on two hidden and dubious assumptions. The first is that because the church is entrusted with the gospel, it can only deal in absolutes: in what is incontrovertibly inherent in the Christian faith. The second is that the church must guard against divisiveness at all costs.

When the first of these assumptions is boldly stated, it

manifestly rests on a confusion between the givenness of the gospel and the interpretation of it. Theological agreement has always been difficult to attain, and the line between what is deemed to be essential and what is subject to revision has invariably been hard to draw. The Roman Catholic Church has sought to resolve the problem by distinguishing between infallible papal pronouncements (which are severely restricted) and those which do not carry this *imprimatur*. But the papacy has never confined itself to the former as the distinction makes plain. The other branches of the Christian church have all tended to identify themselves by an irreducible core of doctrine, but none have managed to exclude theological disagreement; indeed it has increasingly been recognized that the attempt to do so is stultifying, preventing exploration and insight into the deeper truth through creative dialogue. The growth of the ecumenical movement, not least in the Roman Catholic Church since the Second Vatican Council, has led to questioning the whole notion of infallibility and to the common quest for a fuller understanding of the truth as it has been revealed in Jesus and attested to in the scriptures and the tradition of the church. The desire for security in infallible teaching is a natural human impulse, but it contradicts the calling of the pilgrim people of God to venture into a future as yet unknown. Playing safe is not an obvious Christian virtue.

The second assumption is partly true and partly false. The unity of the church is clearly important, but it does not exclude differences. Diverse interpretations of the gospel are not only a fact; they are inevitable if there is to be growth into larger understanding. Nevertheless, people find it hard to tolerate them when they touch their own cherished traditions. This becomes particularly acute when political issues are at stake. Many members of the Church of England, for example, are content to tolerate wide differences of emphasis in matters of doctrine without claiming that these disastrously divide the church, but strongly resent any pronouncement from the pulpit that casts doubt upon their own political allegiance. The gospel calls in question all our cherished views whether they be doctrinal or political, and the unity of the church is tested by our readiness to live with differences, to be open to fresh insights and not to try to turn it into a club of the like-minded.

All the same, Robin Gill has a point. There is a distinction between what the churches are able to say and what the individual Christian or groups of Christians within them are free to advocate. In the former case some degree of consensus is necessary; otherwise the leadership would only speak for itself and not with the support of those it represents. It is possible to be one or even two steps ahead of the rank and file, but not three, four or five; that would mean losing touch with the main body. It is the function of leaders to lead, but not to lose contact with the troops. This means that the churches as institutions will inevitably lag behind their most prophetic voices. To a large extent they are bound by synodical and committee decisions. However, this is not as inhibiting as Robin Gill seems to suggest, nor does it fit into the sharp dichotomy between the priestly and prophetic role. In recent years, for example, the British Council of Churches has exercised increasing influence on questions of foreign policy, defence and race relations, carrying with it a pretty wide consensus of Christian conviction. And however strongly some politicians may have criticized the Archbishop of Canterbury in his attitude to the Falklands conflict and the nuclear threat, Christian opinion has on the whole been behind him.

Nevertheless, if Christian values and principles are to be cashed in terms of policies that are bound to be controversial, this must depend on the advocacy of those who are prepared to take a stand irrespective of whether they are supported by a general consensus or not. This is the calling of every Christian in whatever station of life he finds himself. It is the responsibility of the churches to give a lead to the nation as far as they are able to do so within the limitations imposed upon them as institutions whose members hold diverse views, but they are also charged with providing a context within which policies can be clarified and support given to their members in the discharge of their public obligations.

To sum up. Politics is the sphere of the provisional, or the best that can be achieved in the circumstances, and it is with the theology of the provisional that we have to be concerned. It is easier to deal in absolutes. But when politics is turned into the confrontation of absolutes, with one nation or party claiming a monopoly of the truth, international chaos and social disintegration follow. Similarly, when Christians insist on sticking with theological absolutes, this is a prescription for irrelevance; for the world as it is is not amenable to the final establishment of absolute principles. In turn this leads to the current and disastrous use of the word 'theology' to apply to any abstract argument which has nothing to do with the practical. But if God is concerned with the real world, then the proper business of theology is not a discussion of abstract principles or of doctrines only applicable within ecclesiastical buildings. Its real task is wrestling with the provisional arrangements we have to make in a society in transition, corrupted by sin and confused about ultimate values.

Here the imagery of the Bible is apposite. The human race is lost in the wilderness. The best we can hope for is to pitch our tents in one camp site after another, making the best provisional arrangements we can, looking for that city with foundations whose builder and maker is God. Our provisional arrangements are undergirded by our faith that the end of our pilgrimage is in the hands of God.

That is the context within which we have to work out our politics, whether understood in the narrow sense as policies and programmes of government or in the broader sense of engagement in public life at all levels. We are summoned to hold to the Christian vision and at the same time translate it into the practical possibilities of the society in which we find ourselves.

2

Democracy and Participation

First of all, then, we need to ask some fundamental question about our democratic institutions. In his famous Gettysburg address Abraham Lincoln declared his high resolve 'that this nation, under God, shall have a new birth of freedom; and that government of the people, by the people, and for the people, shall not perish from the earth'. This has been taken to be the basic principle underlying the American constitution and a definitive statement of what true democracy is. I want to begin by asking three questions about it. First, does it represent the way in which government in Britain and in the Western world actually works? Second, is democracy so defined desirable? Third, is it possible to put it into practice?

Without doubt, Abraham Lincoln meant exactly what he said, believing that this was the ideal form of government and that it was possible to achieve it under the American constitution. The outcome has, in fact, been very different. In the United States and Western Europe alike people have been bewitched into supposing that our democratic institutions, for which such high claims have been made, guarantee popular sovereignty in conformity with Lincoln's dream. Gradually it has become apparent that, in spite of the extension of the franchise, effective power rests elsewhere: in the machinery of government, in the military establishment, in the great industrial corporations, in the financial institutions and in the trade unions. Those in positions of influence in these estates of the realm can exercise some leverage on matters of policy, though even this is limited by the complexity of the organizations of which they are part. The ordinary citizen has practically no influence at all. He can cast his vote at national or local elections, but if his candidate is defeated, that is virtually the end of the matter as far as he is concerned. If his candidate wins, this makes very little difference; those elected to office, besides having severely restricted power, immediately become members of an organization from which the voter is excluded. They are all too frequently seen as belonging to *them* rather than to *us*.

Is this an exaggeration? In some respects it is; for it leaves out of account the important differences between Western democracy and totalitarian régimes. The ballot box does provide an ultimate safeguard against the unbridled exercise of power. Politicians at least are accountable to the electorate from time to time for the discharge of their responsibilities, and they have to be sensitive to public opinion throughout their term of office. Moreover, the voters have the opportunity of expressing their preference for one candidate or party rather than another. There is also freedom to protest against policies which are felt to be wrong and the right to organize pressure groups to advocate almost any cause. None of this is possible under totalitarian régimes, or at the most freedom of expression is severely restricted, and those who venture beyond the proscribed bounds are liable to summary arrest.

The importance of this should not in any way be underrated, but it should also not be exaggerated. Those who hold the reins of power are all too prone to minimize the degree to which the average citizen is subject to forces he cannot control and to delude themselves as well as the general public in discounting the range of policy-making which turns out to be the prerogative of the very few. This becomes further complicated when we take into account the phenomenon of what we may call 'organization man': the man who is caught up in a bureaucracy which has its own momentum and built-in constraints. Individuals who are part of the system often feel as powerless as those who are outside it.

Three illustrations may serve to clarify what I have been saying. The peoples of the world want peace, and yet there is an escalating arms race. This cannot be explained simply in terms of a few power-hungry politicians. If it could, they would be quickly dismissed from office; and that applies to the Soviet Union as much as any other country. Behind the leading politicians, there is a vast bureaucracy, including the military establishment and the arms trade, which has a vested interest in keeping its empire intact, with freedom to pursue its own technological goals. In this the average citizen has no voice at all. Even Henry Kissinger is reported to have said that the military establishments of the United States and the Soviet Union are in collusion with one another against the interests of the people of both countries. If this is at all accurate, obviously he did not mean that there is a deliberate conspiracy between them, but that, in pursuing the same goals, they are fuelling one another. The result is a state of affairs which nobody wants. Certainly it is not government of the people, by the people and for the people.

Our own political leaders would doubtless be quick to reply that in this country at least the armed services and the trade which supplies them are under the strict control of the government. But it is not quite as simple as that, grateful as we should be for the measure of control which this implies and the long tradition of independence of political policy which has made our army, navy and air force such highly professional organizations. But we are caught up in the conflict of the super-powers, and it is by no means clear that the military establishments of either the Soviet Union or the United States are devoid of political influence. This is taken for granted as far as the Soviet military machine is concerned, but there is disturbing evidence that the same is true of the Pentagon and the arms trade behind it, though perhaps to not such an obvious or marked degree. The motivation behind this is not military aggression or even defence so much as technological advance and the prestige of the armed services.

There is a built-in mechanism for self-preservation and advancement in every large organization which is subtly resistant to political control. And that is as true of our own military establishment as it is of any other country. I have no doubt that the overwhelming majority of serving officers, scientists, engineers, technicians and managers would say that they do not want war any more than anyone else; and they would be completely sincere in saying so. However, they are caught up in a system not of their own constructing. They came into it, some out of a wish to serve their country, others to earn a salary commensurate with their technical qualifications. They find themselves enmeshed in a huge network which has its own self-justification. It requires overwhelming public opinion and resolute political will to stop the arms race in its tracks and reverse the escalating trend. In the meanwhile, government of the people, by the people and for the people remains a dream.

A second illustration can be taken from the world of industry. It has long been the conventional wisdom that the market is determined by the demands of the consumers. Here at least the ordinary citizen is sovereign by deciding what he or she will buy. In a series of books published since the end of the Second World War, the American economist, John Kenneth Galbraith, has argued that this popular assumption has progressively become obsolete. While it remains true that market forces continue to prevail in small businesses and service industries, they represent only a diminishing sector of the economy, which on both sides of the Atlantic has come to be dominated by governments and the relatively few large industrial corporations. They are not responsive to market forces and consumer choice in the way in which the small entrepreneur is; they set their own targets and the consumer has to abide by the result.

The most startling conclusion which Galbraith draws from his survey of the Western economy is what he sees as the shift from the dominating motive of profit to that of increased production for its own sake, irrespective of whether the commodities produced accord with the needs or wants of the consumer. It is production that counts because, as long as this is expanding, the careers of those engaged in the technostructive (by which Galbraith means the corporate management of the industry) are thereby safeguarded and a road to promotion is assured. The amount of profit is no longer the over-riding consideration. When a company reaches a certain size (and this has happened in the multi-national corporations), the former owners have given place to management; shareholders have virtually no say in matters of policy; employees find themselves the tools of an enterprise over which they have no control; and consumers have to take what they are offered, bamboozled by massive advertising campaigns designed to ensure that the products are sold. Given the long-term investment and planning involved in large corporations, the market has to be controlled. Only a major world economic recession, the possibility of which Galbraith did not sufficiently take into account, can effectively put a brake on such expansion and threaten the technostructure. That is what we have seen happening at the beginning of the 1980s. But it still leaves the ordinary consumer powerless, the victim of forces beyond his or her control.

When we turn to the political scene, we find much the same state of affairs. Local councillors complain that they are in the hands of their officials who in turn say that they are constrained by Whitehall. Backbenchers complain that they have no power over the party machine or the executive, while members of the cabinet have gone on record that they have found themselves prisoners of the civil service. Even the Prime Minister is not as free to take decisions as she is popularly supposed to be. She is dependent on a network of advice in which many public servants have played a part. As in the military establishment and large-scale industry, the individual politician is part of a complex organization which is strongly resistant to pressure for change. If this is the case within it, by how much more is it impervious to influence by the ordinary citizen? It is a far cry from government of the people, by the people or for the people.

These three illustrations serve to underscore the powerlessness of ordinary citizens in the face of those estates of the realm within which decisions are made directly affecting their lives. They reflect their growing sense of alienation from the whole political process, making him feel, as I have said, that those elected to office become members of a caste apart with whose activities he no longer identifies. Everyday speech gives the game away. People commonly refer to 'the council' or 'the government', rarely, if ever, to 'our council' or 'our government'. Public expenditure is seen as something which *they* ought to provide, rates and taxes as impositions to be avoided wherever possible. This is quite illogical, but gut feeling generally over-rides logic, and, whereas everyone on a moment's reflection would have to admit that public provision has to be paid for by ordinary people, common reaction to the obvious discloses a deep underlying feeling of alienation from the political establishment. This is most apparent amongst those who refuse to vote at elections. It is more disturbingly widespread amongst those who do cast their ballot but are increasingly sceptical about the ability of politicians to deliver the promises they make. Abraham Lincoln's dream seems far removed from the way in which our democracy is felt to work.

That being so, it would seem that our next question should be, 'How is the democratic process to be reformed to bring it nearer to the ideal which Lincoln proclaimed?' But first we have to ask whether that is desirable. Not everyone by any manner of means has believed that it is, including many of those who have paid lip service to it. Perhaps the most powerful and influential case against popular democracy was made by Plato in the Athens of the fifth century BC. His famous work, *The Republic*, was written against the background of the decline of his own city-state. He had experienced for himself the corruption of two forms of government – oligarchy and democracy. Oligarchy had been the rule of a select few who had governed in their own selfish interests. Democracy in Athens had taken the form of decision-making by an assembly of all the citizens (the slave population was excluded) and Plato had seen how this could be dominated by a demagogue whose personality and oratory could mesmerize the people and precipitate them into ill-considered action. Therefore he set himself to think out an ideal form of the state, although there is no reason to suppose that he believed it could be put into practice in every detail. He conceived it as an archetype to which any healthy state should seek to conform, realization always inevitably falling short of the ideal.

The theme of *The Republic* is the nature of justice: a word Plato probably used rather than goodness for his purpose because he believed that it covered what he wanted to say about the relation of the individual to society. To realize what he meant by the word, we have to understand that he gave it a broader connotation than the sense in which we commonly use it today. When we speak of justice, we are thinking of a fair distribution of resources and an equitable ordering of social relationships. Plato intended it to embrace what ought to be counted as morally valuable, whether in the individual or in society at large. Indeed, he did not think that the two could be separated: justice or moral value in the individual and in society were interdependent and reflected one another in a proper ordering of parts.

We begin to see what he meant by considering his idea of the good man or, as he put it, of justice in the soul. He had a tripartite view of man's essential nature as consisting of the passions, the spirited element and reason. The passions were the instinctive desires for pleasurable satisfaction. The spirited element was the active, vigorous aspect of human beings, principally expressed in the virtue of courage. Reason was man's intellectual endowment, his capacity for acquiring knowledge and ordering his life in the light of an ideal goal. Everything depended on the proper ordering of these three elements or parts. The good man, the man with justice in his soul, was one in whom the passions were under the control of the spirited in him and both under the control of reason.

After the same fashion Plato believed that for society to be healthy, to be just, it must be hierarchically ordered. At the lowest level were the artisans, the labourers and craftsmen who provided for the material needs of the people: farmers, builders, carpenters, weavers, shoemakers, potters, bakers, etc. Above them were the guardians, trained in military arts and selected through a process of education based on music and gymnastics. From amongst these were to be chosen a small, élite group of potential rulers who were deemed to be capable of protracted and exacting study in mathematics and philosophy with a view to becoming those whose wisdom entitled them to govern. They, and they alone, would not be liable to corruption, because, having apprehended the form of the good and the supreme value of the quest of truth, they would be reluctant to forsake this for the business of ruling the state and would only consent to do so by being persuaded that it was their duty. Thus government was to be in the hands of those whom Plato called philosopher-kings; for such men alone were qualified for the task.

It is interesting to note in passing that Plato prescribed a rigorous communal life for his guardians which was to prove the seed-bed for the selection of those destined to be philosopher-kings. While there is no suggestion that the artisans should not marry as they wished, raise families, own their own property and pursue their own interests as most of them did in fifth-century Athens, the guardians were to be placed under the strictest discipline. They would not be allowed to own any property, their needs being supplied by the rest of the community. This, Plato believed, would prevent them being diverted to private interests from their responsibility for the common good.

Marriages were to be arranged to ensure the procreation of the most gifted children from amongst whom the next generation of guardians and rulers would be recruited. They would not be left to their parents, but would be the responsibility of this élite community for their training and education from which they would be downgraded to the artisan class if they did not show sufficient promise. Boys and girls, women and men would be subjected to exactly the same discipline – music and gymnastics and learning the arts of war – and females would be expected to go into battle, if required to do so, on an equal footing with males. There was, in general, to be no sex distinction amongst the guardians, other than the acknowledgement that women and girls were weaker than men and boys. This may have been the reason why Plato apparently did not envisage the possibility of women rulers; there is no mention of philosopher-queens in the *The Republic*!

The ideal city was to be governed in accordance with the values that the rulers had learned to appreciate through their mathematical and philosphical studies. Accordingly, Plato advocated a wide-ranging censorship of literature and the arts with a view to excluding anything that was likely to mislead the young or persuade them to admire what was untruthful, ignoble, ugly or base. Some of the great names in Greek literature and drama came in for rough handling on this count, and Plato went so far as to propose the censorship of the works of men of genius like Homer and Sophocles. It is not that he underrated them as poets, dramatists and artists, but he thought much of their work was dangerous if the ideals in which he believed were to be formative in the best of all possible states.

Having portrayed the ideal structure of society as he conceived it, in the eighth book of the *The Republic* Plato proceeded to compare five types of government, ranging them in an order of what might be called degeneration. At the top was the aristocratic, the rule of the best men, the élite chosen not on the basis of their popularity or recruited from the ambitious, but in virtue of their character and ability. Second came the timocratic or honour- seeking state in which rulers had become obsessed with their own importance and had combined with the guardians to confiscate the property of the rest of the citizens and divide it amongst themselves. This would lead to the pursuit of wealth and the rise of oligarchy or government by the few, motivated not by the spirit of public service, but by the selfish desire to accumulate riches at the expense of the community. Those so deprived and oppressed would in the end revolt, take over the reins of power and establish a democracy, the rule of the people. But since they would have neither the knowledge nor the ability nor the training to exercise such responsibility, they would be open to the blandishments of any demagogue who came along, and tyranny would result. Thus Plato set aristocracy over against tyranny as the poles between which the government of any state oscillates. 'Just as the philosopher, in whom reason rules, is the happiest of men, so the aristocratic state is the best and happiest of states; and just as the tyrannical despot, the slave of ambition and passion, is the worst and most unhappy of men, so is the state ruled by the tyrant the worst and most unhappy of States.'[1]

This survey of different types of government is not intended by Plato to be a historical sketch, but rather an indication of how the best ordering of society can easily degenerate into something worse and ultimately end in disaster. He was under no illusions about the precarious nature of any social structure. He could hardly have been otherwise in the light of his experience at Athens. But he believed that the only way in which to secure the recovery of his own city-state and indeed provide for a just society anywhere else was to set the ideal before all who would listen and warn them against the perils of departing from it.

Much of this may at first seem remote from our concern with the modern nation-state and the complexity of industrial society. Admittedly, the setting is very different, and Plato could not possibly have foreseen the problems that would arise on the large scale with which we are familiar. The city-states of Greece numbered only a few thousand in their population, though they were surrounded by the great empires of the ancient world. All the same, when we stop to reflect, we can see that the *The Republic* raises many questions which have a very contemporary ring about them. Can there be a healthy state which has discounted all sense of ultimate values and rests upon the collective aspirations of its individual citizens? Is there a way of making democracy work which does not deliver decisions into the hands of a power-seeking minority? How is the lust for power to be controlled anyway? Is the ideal of human equality a realistic one, given the innate differences between people in terms of natural ability, insight and training? Is there a case for élitism? Is there an argument for eugenics if the quality of leadership really matters? How far is the possession of private property a guarantee of freedom or how far is it inevitably a source of injustice and an obstacle to government for the common good? What is the proper relationship between the sexes? How are the rights and opportunities of women to be safeguarded? What is the place of the family in a healthy society? Is there a case for censorship to preserve and foster the standards of a given society?

The case for élitism and a hierarchical form of government has prevailed in various forms right down to the present day: the doctrine of the divine right of kings in the time of the Stuarts and the claims made for the papacy in the mediaeval period, to take but two examples. In more recent times it has been adopted by the followers of Karl Marx, notably by Lenin in his development of the role of the communist party. It is the party which is entrusted with the truth, which alone understands what is in the interests of the people as a whole. Accordingly, democracy has been redefined in Eastern Europe not as government *by* the people, but government *for* the people. The population as a whole is not to be trusted to know what is in its best interests – what should be done if it really understood; the party alone is competent to speak and act for the nation. The Western democracies have, of course, rejected this claim, but not altogether. The nineteenth-century tradition of aristocratic government still has deep roots within British Conservatism today and the more extreme elements in the Labour Party follow the same path in reverse. Insisting that the activists in the constituency caucuses should determine policy, with scant attention paid to the mass of Labour supporters, they pursue a campaign of excluding from influence any who do not toe their own line. Even Harold Wilson, in proclaiming that the Labour party was now the natural party of government, was in danger of having this interpreted as meaning that it could speak for the whole nation, when in fact it represented only a minority of the electorate. 'Big brother knows best' still has its advocates in many guises. Democracy means government *for* the people, not *by* the people.

Now values are clearly at stake here, and Christians need to think out where they stand in the light of the biblical revelation. Plato's thesis is a very persuasive one, resting as it does on three pillars which are solidly based in experience: people do not have equal capacity or insight; the crowd is easily swayed by a demagogue and can quickly become a destructive force; a society which is not governed by justice understood in terms of moral ideals is bound to lapse into tyranny. I do not see how these propositions can be controverted. History bears overwhelming testimony to them. We have only to think of the excesses of the French revolution at the end of the eighteenth century or, more recently, the ravages caused by the appeal to popular emotion in Nazi Germany. But does this make out a shut and closed case for élitism, and has Lincoln's promise to be dismissed as an idealistic dream?

Three Christian insights are relevant in answering this question. In the first place, there is a crucially important qualification in Lincoln's famous declaration: 'this nation, *under God*, shall have a new birth of freedom'. Remove the words underlined and you have a prescription for popularism. For the founding fathers of the American constitution, the inclusion of subservience to the purpose of God was no polite acknowledgement of religion as having a place in the nation's life; it undergirded the democracy which they sought to establish. Secularism on both sides of the Atlantic has undermined that, making government of the people, by the people, and for the people such a man-centred ideal as to threaten the very coherence of society. Plato would have agreed in principle with the founding fathers, even though he would have expressed his agreement in different terms. Unless people at large accept a set of values for the shaping of their society, disintegration is inevitable, and the kind of values they are prepared to accept will determine the sort of society that will emerge.

Here the Christian parts company with Plato. He believed, as we have seen, that irresponsible populism could be avoided only by training an èlite of philosopher-kings who would pursue the ideal of the good with complete disinterestedness. The Christian analysis of the human condition denies that there are such people, immune from the frailties and temptations which limit everyone else. The acquisition of power carries with it the tendency to corruption; and the more power anyone has, the more he or she becomes disposed to arrogance and the dismissal of opposition as tiresome frustration. A common characteristic of human nature is the difficulty we find in admitting that we may be wrong, and that is certainly a marked feature of politicians. Yes, some people are better than others, some more gifted than others, some more to be trusted with responsibility than others. None is free of the need for correction. This is in part supplied by colleagues and advisers, but they inevitably belong to a closed circle with its own built-in resistance to outside interference. That is why it is important to ensure that the means of affecting policy is as widely distributed as possible. The voice of the people is not the voice of God, but it is more likely to restrain unbridled power than any other influence that can be exerted. Moreover, for the health of any society the government needs the support of the population at large.

In the third place, central to the Christian understanding of man is the belief that every individual should be given the fullest possible opportunity to develop his own potentiality, however limited that may be. People must not be treated as cyphers, manipulated to fit in to some pattern or policy devised from above, nor is their integrity respected by having things done for them, when the business of government should be to provide the conditions in which they can decide for themselves what they can and ought to do. This has practical consequences for the devolution of responsibility to which I shall come in a moment. Here I am making the point that Lincoln's dictum has to be taken as a whole: democracy in the full meaning of the word is only government *for* the people when it is *by* the people.

But is it practicable? Obviously it is not, if the ideal is taken to mean that everyone should have a say in every governmental decision that affects his or her life. In the modern world that would be a prescription for total paralysis. During the Cromwellian period such an interpretation of democracy was seriously advocated by the Levellers, drawing on their experience of the way in which decisions were reached in their independent conventicles. At the famous army council at Putney in 1647 their spokesmen insisted that all laws should have the consent of those to whom they applied and that it was contrary to the Christian understanding of man that anyone should assume the right to impose his will on anyone else. 'The poorest he hath a life to live as the richest he,' declared Colonel Rainboro, drawing the conclusion that the rich and the privileged should not be allowed to legislate for the poor. All were equal in the sight of God, and therefore all should have an equal say in the regulations affecting their lives. Oliver Cromwell and his son-in-law, Henry Ireton, replied that this was simply not practical politics. Cromwell was sympathetic to the aspirations of the Levellers and shared their religious convictions, but he knew too much about the problems of government to be able to accept the demands they were making; and Ireton was even more adamant.

The significance of this debate can hardly be over-emphasised. The late Lord Lindsay held that it sowed the seeds of modern democracy, leading ultimately to the extension of the franchise and raising the questions which are still unresolved.[2] Following the General Election of 1979, the case argued by the Levellers has once again come to the forefront in the controversy which has split the Labour Party. Should the annual conference through its executive committee dictate the manifesto and control government policy after an election has been won, and should members of Parliament be accountable to their constituency parties for the way in which they vote in the lobbies of the House of Commons? Tony Benn has been at the centre of the debate and is something of an enigma. On the one hand his writings and speeches show that he has been profoundly influenced by the Levellers. He claims, with a great deal of justification, that the modern Prime Minister has more power than a mediaeval monarch, that the executive needs to be made more accountable to Parliament and that the party in power should be responsible to the annual conference and, through it, to the constituency parties and the trade unions. He claims – and, I believe, sincerely – that he wants to extend democracy as far as possible by opening the doors of the cabinet office and the civil service departments. On the other hand, he has allowed himself to be dragged on the coat-tails of the extreme Left, whose notion of democracy differs very little from that of Lenin. Tony Benn has simply not answered the question how he would propose to democratize the party caucuses and the trade unions.

He knows that he would meet resistance there and possibly thinks that his proposals go as far as is practicable at the present time. But that leaves the lurking suspicion that he is not prepared to face the fact that party activists and trade union leaders do not obviously represent the people for whom they are supposed to speak. Benn's democracy, however well-intended – and I am prepared to give him the benefit of the doubt – founders at the point where it stops. There it slips all too easily into the Leninist position that the party, defined in terms of the self-styled orthodox, acts for the interests of the people, whether the people recognize it or not.

The reaction of most of those with experience of government is much the same as that of Cromwell and Ireton to the Levellers: those entrusted with political responsibility have a duty to use their best judgment in the light of facts which cannot be equally available to or at the discretion of everybody. To take perhaps the most controversial example, there is little doubt that a plebiscite would produce a large majority in favour of the restoration of capital and corporal punishment. The House of Commons has repeatedly refused to do so. Why? Because many members of Parliament believe that in the light of information available to them they are in a better position to judge what is in the public interest. Others – a minority – disagree. Hence the substantial vote in favour of hanging and flogging. But if a majority consistently takes the view it does on a subject on which it is at least plausible to argue that popular opinion is as well-informed as those who have the responsibility for passing legislation, by how much more is the case for privileged discretion strengthened in all those many matters of policy on which the general public cannot possibly be expected to have an informed judgment?

The question can be carried further. We have hardly yet come to terms with the vast changes that have taken place since the end of the Second World War as a result of which the absolute sovereignty of the nation state has been progressively eroded, if not made obsolete. The complexities of world trade, the international monetary system and the growth of multi-national corporations have decisively removed the centre of economic policy-making from the governments of the various countries. The European Economic Community with its headquarters in Brussels and its parliament at Strasbourg has already taken over responsibilities which over-ride purely national interests, and the instruments of the United Nations, like the World Health Organization, have provided means of co-operation for tackling global problems which no national government could hope to solve. The weaknesses of these relatively new structures are the inevitable teething-troubles of a divided world and reflect the resistance of policitians of all countries to surrendering anything of their cherished independence, but they point the only way forward to the peace and prosperity of all mankind. When Enoch Powell, Michael Foot and others cry 'Halt' in the name of the sovereignty of Parliament, they are simply trying to put the clock back, to return to an unrealistic dream of a self-contained island.

As these international organizations gain in strength and recognition – and they must if civilization is to survive – their remoteness from the ordinary citizen will become an inescapable fact. How can the average man or woman in the street be expected to have any influence at all on such large-scale operations? Those directly engaged will inevitably be people of special ability, recruited for service in a highly complex structure. Set against this the very limited interest, experience, knowledge and understanding of the average person, and Lincoln's dream seems totally unrealistic.

Is that the end of the matter? Do we have to admit that democracy is simply unworkable and that we have to abandon the idea altogether? I do not believe so, but we do have to rethink what we mean by it and free it from the misuses to which it is so often put. That implies starting with ordinary people where they are and asking how they may most effectively take responsibility for decisions that affect their lives.

First of all, they, and they alone, can say where the shoe pinches. The metaphor is one which A. D. Lindsay often used in his lectures to undergraduates when explaining the fundamental principles of democratic government. If you want a new pair of shoes, he said, you go to the shoemaker. You do not tell him how to make them. That is his business. But, when he delivers them, it is for you to say whether or not they pinch your feet. If they do, you tell him to try again. So with government at every level. It is the prerogative of the electorate in any democracy to reject the policies of legislators and the way in which they are implemented if what they do is unacceptable. That is the ultimate sanction against the exercise of unbridled power.

Second, this is not simply negative. If the electorate has the right to say what is unacceptable, it also has the responsibility to set priorities consistent with the kind of society in which it wishes to live. Here values are at stake and the attitudes of ordinary people are of the utmost importance. If the priority is for everyone to raise their material standard of living, and if this means it is to be done at any expense to other people, then we shall have the acquisitive society, and governments will be judged by their success or failure in fulfilling the demands made upon them. If we believe that competition should over-ride co-operation in the way in which we are related to one another, the result will be a scrambling for advantage in the rat race. If our major objective is to defend what we have at all costs, then we shall have a siege economy and a nationalistic approach to military expenditure. These attitudes have become deeply ingrained in the mass of the British people, and it is no use blaming the government, whichever party is in power, if the result is a disintegrating society. We get the government we deserve.

Christian priorities are in sharp contrast to those outlined in the preceding paragraph, and they are shared by many who do not profess the Christian faith. The quality of life takes precedence over the quest for money and possessions. The elimination of poverty and deprivation far outweighs securing material advantages for the successful. Co-operation and a sense of mutual responsibility should replace competition as the basic principle of our industrial and commercial life. The search for peace should have the urgency which is currently channelled into defence.

It is for Christians and all who share these values to make their influence felt as widely as possible. If they do, there is the prospect of having an impact on government policies in a positive direction. An example springs to mind as I write from the spectacular growth of the peace movement. Behind the controversial campaign for unilateral nuclear disarmament lies the passionate desire of ordinary people for those in government to do something effective to halt the arms race and avert a holocaust. It is as if a tidal wave of popular conviction was forcing governments in the

East and the West alike to bring fresh urgency to their task. Almost in desperation masses of people are virtually saying, 'Stop playing games with our lives and the lives of our children. Don't leave the conference room without making progress.' In the last resort the significance of the peace movement is not the campaign for unilateral nuclear disarmament, but the demand of ordinary people for the statesmen of the world to make peace. And it is having an effect. The test will come if talks break down. Will popular pressure begin to evaporate?

In the third place, we need to begin to rethink the distribution of power and responsibility between the various levels of government. In discussing élitism I have already argued that the Christian understanding of human nature emphasizes the sinfulness and fallibility of everyone, whoever they may be. Those entrusted with power and responsibility, however able, are prone to corruption by the very offices they hold, and therefore need checks and balances to counteract this all-pervasive human weakness, striking evidence for which is the reluctance of politicians and civil servants alike to suffer any diminuation of their sphere of influence. A tendency to empire building is the rule rather than the exception. Therefore, the more widely responsibility is distributed the better.

Resistance to this invariably accompanies the enlargement and centralization of government agencies. The two go hand in hand, and efficiency is invoked to defend the concentration of power. What this often means is that administrative convenience becomes the accepted principle for deciding the structure of an organization. But that is a value judgment, rarely recognized as such, and open to serious challenge. It is by no means self-evident that this should be an over-riding consideration, especially when it leads to too much power being in the hands of too few people. Nor is administrative convenience necessarily efficient. It may well result in bureaucratic paralysis. Mistakes may be avoided, but very little achieved.

Government has grown like Topsy, often with makeshift divisions of responsibility, resulting in half thought-out compromises. All too rarely is the question asked 'What is the basis for deciding who should do what?' Commenting on the changes that have taken place over recent years in the distribution of governmental responsibilities, Max Beloff and Gillian Peele argue that 'this perpetual mutation – which has affected local authorities and regional administrative agencies as well as central departments – has been inspired by no clear principles, so that there is frequently no yardstick against which to measure the success of any changes'.[3] It is, therefore, hardly surprising that there is a widespread sense that too many decisions are taken by the wrong people in the wrong places, illustrated by the growing tension between central and local government and the demand for devolution of powers to the regions, and to Scotland and Wales in particular.

But it is necessary to consider devolution in more than one direction. When the word is used, it is commonly thought to refer only to the delegation of powers from central government to the regions, the districts and the local communities. We are now living in a world, as we have seen, where we have to take seriously the devolution of responsibility from national governments to international agencies. This is the theme of an important book by two Americans, Gerald and Patricia Mische.[4] They argue for the decreasing role of the nation state, some of the functions of which should be taken over by international organizations and others transferred to small communities. They believe that a more human world order depends on escaping from what they call 'The National Security Straightjacket', and for them, that means balancing the international agencies with greatly strengthened local government and community responsibility. Given the upsurge of aggressive nationalism in the modern world, this at first looks like an idealistic pipe-dream. But we are going to be driven to take it seriously; for even limited progress towards it is the one way forward to a world where people can live in peace and find fulfilment in communities to which they can significantly relate.

This is too large an issue and raises too many questions of detail to be dealt with in a few paragraphs. The point I am making is the general one: that devolution of responsibility should be the governing principle rather than centralization in the interests of administrative convenience, because the latter means dangerous concentration of power whereas the former allows for its distribution.

The acceptance of this principle carries with it one important corollary. If we are bound to acknowledge, as we must, that democracy works only when responsibility is delegated – and that is what representative government means – it is crucially important that those elected to office should be trusted. They should be felt by the people who vote for them to be their representatives, charged with doing on their behalf what they cannot do for themselves. That relationship of trust has been breaking down, as I have maintained, between members of Parliament and their constituents and between local councillors and their electors. This sense of alienation is in no small measure due to confusion about what they could and should be doing on behalf of those they represent. If they are caught up in a confused system themselves, they are hardly to be blamed for failing to deliver what the average citizen expects. Our machinery of government is in drastic need of overhaul.

Finally, we come back to where I started: with ordinary men and women in the families, associations and communities where they live and work. After all, they constitute the body politic. Few of them will become political activists. Nor should we expect it. They are concerned with their homes, their children, their jobs, their gardens, their leisure activities; they meet in social clubs, in pubs, in voluntary societies of all kinds; they gossip with neighbours and friends, often preoccupied with the tensions and tangles of human relationships. That is what life is all about, not the debates of the political parties on the local council or in the House of Commons. The decisions taken there are necessary to provide the context in which ordinary people may live out their lives together. That is the business of those who are elected to public office: to keep the peace, to maintain law and order, to ensure safeguards against fires and natural disasters, to provide water supplies, sewerage, roads, transport and basic standards of public health. These are essential requirements for an infrastructure of living together in community. Beyond this there has been general agreement that the state should take responsibility for education, comprehensive health care and a wide range of social services. But, however far this is extended, it can provide only the context for day-to-day living, and even the most convinced advocates of public provision are having to recognize that there are limits to what government can do.

A wide field for debate remains about what should constitute the desirable context or infrastructure of a healthy society. However, the onus of proof rests on those who would multiply statutory responsibilities. The criterion should be that nothing is to be attemped by national or local government which the neighbourhood is capable of organizing or providing for itself; and in that church congregations have a significant part to play. A vigorous democracy depends on giving responsibility to ordinary people, and so there should be the maximum encouragement for voluntary initiative in the community; for only then will the wealth of local talent be fully harnessed. That was the theme of the last programme in Ralph Dahrendorf's television series on Britain. He gave three examples of community enterprises (not necessarily the most aptly chosen or portrayed) in which he saw hopeful signs of the way in which this country might emerge from the doldrums and look to a more creative future. We have to begin at the grass roots, where people actually are, building society from the ground upwards. As Jo Grimond has repeatedly argued, Britain is over-governed, and, when that is so, it cannot be government of the people, by the people or for the people.

3

Party Games and the Establishment

In Gilbert and Sullivan's *Iolanthe* the sentry outside the Houses of Parliament morosely sings how comical it is

> That nature always does contrive
> That every boy and every gal
> That's born into the world alive,
> Is either a little Liberal
> Or else a little Conservative.

After the First World War, when Labour took the place of the Liberals, the same tradition of two-party allegiance survived, most people brought up to believe that they belonged to one camp or the other, seeing politics as a ding-dong battle between government and opposition, with victors and losers changing places as fortune favoured not necessarily the brave, but those whose propaganda most effectively swayed the relatively small proportion of floating voters.

All that has changed in recent years, with traditional ties becoming weaker and the electorate much more volatile. The rise of a third force in the Liberal-SDP Alliance has threatened to put an end to the two-party game and to break the mould of British politics. Whether it will succeed in doing so remains to be seen. It may take a long time; for there are strong vested interests in keeping the game going without changing the rules.

A game it seems to be. When I was a boy at school you were identified with Oxford or Cambridge as the time of the annual boat race drew near. Nowadays the young and many of the not-so-young are more likely to label themselves supporters of Manchester United or Liverpool. Party politics have become very much like that, though I suspect that the great majority of people are a good deal less excited about the outcome of elections than by the result of the Wembley Cup Final, the football scores on Saturday evening or the winners of the day's races. All the same, they look at it as a sort of gladiatorial contest, encouraged to do so by the broadcast of proceedings in Parliament and the way in which the press, radio and television treat the public opinion polls much as they do the league tables in the sports columns of the daily papers. The important issues at stake tend to be submerged by the question 'Who will win?'

Nevertheless, it is policy that really matters, not personalities or popular ratings. Anyone who takes his civic responsibilities seriously has to make up his mind which party to support as elections approach, however dissatisfied he may be with the way in which the game is played. This should apply to every Christian, though, for reasons which will become clear as we proceed, different conclusions are likely to be reached by different people.

There is, however, general agreement that Christians have a duty to vote. Dissatisfaction with the party game or the argument that no party embodies what are conceived to be Christian ideals does not carry conviction. Abstention is a retreat from taking responsible decisions. We do not live in a world where all the options are clear-cut, where ethical decisions are unambiguous. We have to take things as we find them, doing the best we can and prepared, as I have maintained before, to admit that we may be mistaken. A Christian should never refuse to become involved in the political process for fear of being compromised. That is cowardice, not a stand for principle.

Many Christians stop there, convinced that they should vote, but then deciding how to cast their ballot for much the same reasons as anyone else. Not a few are motivated by traditional habit; others influenced by the superficial impressions created by the media. It would be interesting to find out how many could explain or defend the way they vote on the basis of the Christian convictions they profess. The result of a survey carried out in an average congregation would provide much food for thought; but it is unlikely that consent would be given for such an exercise; the secrecy of the ballot box would almost certainly be invoked, concealing embarrassed confusion rather than evidence of standing for Christian principles.

A number of factors explain the confusion to which I have just referred. Many people are sensitive about being asked to question their political allegiance. It is more comfortable to be left alone to nurse one's prejudices without having to bring them into the open. As we grow older, we tend to become more resistant to change, and if we have never made the attempt to relate our politics to our Christian faith, the suggestion that we should do so is disturbing. Furthermore, it requires us to ask where our ultimate loyalty lies: to the party to which we are supposed to belong or to the Lord whom we profess to serve. Not a little of the emotional reaction against what is regarded as the intrusion of the church into politics derives from a quite natural fear of exposure to such a question. It is easier to live life in compartments than to bring the whole of it under the scrutiny of the gospel.

However, there are other and more substantial reasons for avoiding the question. As I have argued in an earlier chapter, political policies inevitably belong to the sphere of the relative; they have to do with the application of values to the complexity of what is practical and often to the choice between alternative methods of achieving agreed ends. Christians have long been conditioned to believe that they can deal only in absolutes, in dogmatic assertions that this or that is the authoritative will of God. When this is seen not to apply to the controversies of party politics, the conclusion is drawn that the latter are neutral from the religious point of view. They can be settled on what appear to be their own merits, divorced from any judgment in the light of ultimate values. That is an extremely difficult position to hold when it is obvious that the ordering of human relationships is at stake, but it derives such plausibility as it has from this ingrained belief, for which the church has been responsible, that the gospel is concerned solely with the eternal, unchanging, unambiguous will of God. Once that is seen to be false, once the doctrine of the Incarnation is taken seriously as the involvement of God in the transitory affairs of human life, the relativities of politics are seen to be the sphere of his continuing activity. The divorce between the absolute and the relative becomes untenable in the sense that

God takes upon himself involvement in the ambiguities of mortal existence. It is often difficult for the Christian to decide what policy or what party he should support in the light of the faith he holds. He is not thereby absolved from making the decision.

The difficulty in doing so is further compounded by the way in which programmes are put together in shaping a manifesto. Anyone who is prepared to take a stand on Christian principles and abandon unequivocal loyalty to a particular party will find himself faced with a mixture of policies some of which have more claim on him than others. For example, at the time of writing the Labour Party is committed by Conference resolutions to unilateral disarmament, withdrawal from the European Economic Community and extension of state control over private industry. Some may feel that their commitment to the first of these is of such over-riding importance that they must vote Labour at the next election, even though they are opposed to withdrawal from Europe and the expansion of government bureaucracy. Others may believe that Conservative defence policy is the best insurance against a nuclear war and that this takes precedence over their doubts about the party's economic strategy and attitude to the Welfare State. The examples could be multiplied, illustrating the fact that even with three major parties the options are severely limited. Individuals are unlikely to find themselves faced with what would be the best possible manifesto, and that is inherent in the compromise which inevitably results from the process by which it comes to be compiled. If there was any doubt about the relativity of all political programmes, this alone would settle it.

Christians may be perplexed not only by the contents and balance of the several manifestoes promulgated by the political parties. They may live in constituencies where the choice of candidates presents them with a dilemma. Someone of obvious integrity may be standing for election against opponents who appear to be mere party sycophants or else lack personal qualities calculated to inspire trust as the best representative of the electorate; and yet they may be standing for one of the parties which offers a programme which seems to be more consistent with Christian principles. What is to be done? Is the vote to be cast for the candidate or the party? Some would think that the answer is obvious, but it will not appear so to everyone; and it is certainly a matter on which Christians are entitled to differ.

If these were not problems enough, there is a further difficulty which stems directly from the way in which the party game is actually played. In order to keep it going and preserve the arena of conflict, both government and opposition have to pretend that each side is absolutely in the right and the other absolutely in the wrong. In other words, the dogmatism which Christians are called upon to renounce when they become politically involved is transferred to the battle on the hustings, to the House of Commons and the council chamber.

Anyone can see on a moment's reflection that this is a sham. There are real differences of philosophy and policy between the various parties, but there is a larger measure of agreement between them than they find it convenient to admit. Any number of examples come to mind, but two will suffice. At the time of writing the Thatcher administration is being blamed for the tragic escalation of unemployment in Britain, though the opposition knows full well that it is due in large measure to factors over which the present government has no control: the economic recession which is affecting all the industrialized countries, and the failure of successive administrations, together with management and trade unions, to face the necessary adjustments to British industry in the light of changing patterns of world trade. The Thatcher government has to deal with the legacies of the past, and so would the Labour Party or the Alliance, if they were holding office. Admittedly, there are sharp differences of opinion about how the crisis should be tackled, but these are magnified at the expense of any admission of past errors and frank acknowledgement of the inherent problems which any government would have to face. An example of the reverse side of the coin is the Conservative insistence on belief in the free market and castigation of the Labour opposition for advocating state intervention in industry, when this is precisely the policy it has had to adopt in regard to Rolls-Royce, British Leyland, the steel industry and shipbuilding. There is a much greater degree of overlap between all the political parties than the rules of the game allow them to admit. When this is seen, it makes the choice faced by the ordinary voter that much more ambiguous.

When all these considerations are taken together, it becomes clear that a case can be made out for choosing to support any of the three major political coalitions; for that is what all three are, based on compromises between those who hold many diverse views. On general grounds it can be argued that the Conservative commitments to free enterprise and curbing the functions of the state allow for the development of individual initiative and with it greater possibilities of human fulfilment. On the other hand, the Labour Party's insistence on corporate responsibility and the role of government in ensuring a fair distribution of wealth and opportunity appeals to values inherent in the gospel. Again, the internationalist stance of the Alliance and its emphasis on co-operation and devolution of powers may persuade others that this more nearly approximates to Christian ideals. These are all general grounds for supporting one party or another. But all the political programmes have many specific proposals on education, health, welfare, employment and so on which may commend themselves with different degrees of persuasiveness to the Christian voter.

All this may seem to suggest that it does not greatly matter which party we support. Such a conclusion would betray superficiality and be profoundly mistaken. Behind the party games and the compromises of the manifestoes fundamental value questions are at stake: sometimes concealed, sometimes half-hidden, more often confused because they are insufficiently exposed to criticism. Whatever the merits of particular policies advanced by the Tory party, the whole approach is governed by the assumption that the pursuit of private self-advancement is to be encouraged and commended, in the name of individual freedom and enterprise, whereas co-operative action in the interests of the community is a dangerous policy to be sparingly implemented, at best designed to fill the gaps and provide a safety-net for those who would otherwise be seriously disadvantaged. Qualifications have to be introduced to meet the obvious needs for a social and economic infrastructure without which society could not function, but the underlying emphasis is on individual initiative: 'the belief that human beings separately are endowed with potential for good, but collectively are full of depravity.'[1] Such an attitude is in sharp contrast with the Christian view of man as made for community. To put it as bluntly as possible, the capitalist system, in so far as it is based on the premise of individual profit and self-advancement at the expense of others, sanctifies selfishness and contradicts the basic Christian conviction that man's fulfilment lies in mutual responsibility for his fellows.

Here a warning is in place. What I have just said is open to misunderstanding and liable to distract attention from the point I am making. Capitalism is a slippery word. Sometimes I have found myself wondering whether it is any longer useful since its meaning has become so ill-defined. It is often treated as a sort of garbage can into which everything is dumped to which people are opposed. A loose bandying about of the word may generate heat, but it is not the source of much light. The modern organization of industry and the economy is very different from anything Karl Marx encountered or sought to overturn. The profit of the industrial magnate and the entrepreneur has to a large extent been replaced by returns on investments expected by big institutions like the pension funds or to a lesser extent on savings by large numbers of ordinary people. The system is now more complex than its most vociferous critics of the Left are often prepared to recognize. In any case, capital, defined as the sum total of land, plant, machinery and labour, is inescapably there. The question is what to do with it; and that brings us back to the purpose for which it is used. I was careful to say that 'the capitalist system, *in so far as it is based on the premise of individual profit and self-advancement at the expense of others*, sanctifies selfishness'. That is the problem, and it is that attitude, rooted in Tory philosophy, which is repugnant to the Christian conscience.

Of course, as I have already argued, Christians should know better than anyone else that selfishness is deeply ingrained in human nature. It is sheer utopianism to think that it can be eradicated by changes in the economic system. But if selfishness is made the touchstone and standard for human endeavour rather than the problem that has to be countered, the most destructive consequences are bound to follow. When individual self-advancement at the expense of other people is sanctified by the government of the day over against corporate action to ensure maximum mutual responsibility, then it is not surprising that everyone follows suit. Trade unionists battle for higher wages at the expense of the pensioner, the lower paid and the unemployed; the disadvantaged take to the streets to demand a decent living standard for themselves; and those who cannot get what they want mug and steal. It is all part of a common syndrome. There is a deeply disturbing connexion between the values being upheld by the Tory Party and the rising incidence of crime. The demand for a larger and more effective police force is like calling for fire engines to extinguish flames which are being stoked with vast quantities of oil.

That is why I believe that modern Conservatism is ultimately incompatible with Christian values; not because of the detailed policies being advocated about which there is plenty of room for debate, but because of the basic philosophy underlying them. If it were to continue to hold the field, the long-term outlook for Britain would be bleak indeed. We should have an increasingly divided, disruptive and decaying society.

The clear-cut alternative to conservative individualism has been the *raison d'être* of the Labour Party and the trade unions. While the Tories sometimes make explicit their fundamental assumptions and sometimes cloak them under the veneer of political pragmatism, Socialists unambiguously take their stand for corporate responsibility. That has always been their real strength, derived from the idealism of their founding fathers, many of whom drew their inspiration from the Christian faith. Their goal was a society in which all would find fulfilment, poverty and exploitation would be eliminated, and everyone would work together for the common welfare: in short, the brotherhood of man.

Tragically, it must be confessed, the dream has faded. Only the pretence remains. For many, the grinding poverty and the harsh working conditions have disappeared, to be replaced by material affluence far beyond the expectations of those of earlier generations. But the quality of life has in many respects deteriorated. Old communities have been broken up; family ties have been weakened; a sense of social purpose has been lost. Worst of all, the ethics of self-interested capitalism have been embraced by so many of those who have inherited the fruits of past struggles. The quest for more money and more and more consumer goods has become the main motivation, often at the expense of those who have failed in the rat race, left behind in the ghettos of the inner cities, the dreary tenements and the spreading pools of the disadvantaged and unemployed.

The story is vividly told in Jeremy Seabrook's account of *What Went Wrong*. Based on an extensive survey of working-class districts in all parts of the country and numerous conversations with people of all ages, the picture emerges of widespread disillusionment with the achievements of the Labour and trade union movements. Things have taken the place of people, who are identified not by what they are, but by what they possess. Mesmerized by the tawdry goods in the shop window and the glamorous advertisements on television, the victims of the consumer society are daily being encouraged to buy more than they have, and when the have it, find themselves unsatisfied and frustrated. Children are loaded with expensive toys and extravagant pocket money because they have to have what they want; and this has become a substitute for the old family relationships and the mutual concern of people for one another. 'The child tends to be stripped of all social influences but those of the market-place; all sense of place, function and class is weakened, the characteristics of region and clan, neighbourhood or kindred are attenuated. The individual is denuded of everything but appetites, desires and tastes, wrenched from any context of human obligation or commitment.'[2] The result of this is that people become alienated from one another; their attachments are to things, not to their fellow human beings. Seabrook sums up his findings as follows: 'If you talk to old working-class people, however oppressive the poverty and insecurity under which they lived, they will always recall that the greatest consolation was the quality of the human relationships; how comforting it was to share, with kin, neighbours, work companions. But now, in the face of the vast improvements in material conditions, it is the people who are wrong. Things are better; but all that has been gained at the expense of human relationships.'[3]

Generalizations of this kind can always be faulted by appealing to exceptions. Vigorous and cohesive working-class communities continue to persist amongst the coal miners, to take a particularly obvious example, though even their traditional solidarity has become eroded through productivity deals offering high bonuses to those who can earn them. Whatever the exceptions, however, there can be no doubt that the values of an acquisitive society have taken deep root in the Labour movement, and the Party has presented itself as the universal provider. 'Put us in power and we will give you what you want.' If that has not been the explicit slogan during election campaigns, it has been the implicit promise. Hence the exaggerated claims for government and the centralization of power which bedevil the Socialist appeal to the electorate.

This is the real weakness of the Labour Party. Instead of breaking down the barriers of class and delivering from dependence those who in former times were exploited and deprived of human dignity, in practice it has failed to encourage the emergence of genuine community in which people share responsibility for the common good. The idea of government as the great provider has taken over, with those elected to office nationally and locally arrogating to themselves the role of the Lady Bountiful. The result has been a massive decline in party membership and a surrender to the standards of an acquisitive society in which the strong fight for advantage over the weak.

This is a travesty of the ideals of the founding fathers and makes the Conservative case for individual initiative attractive by comparison. But it is a travesty which many in the Labour Party would reject. The old idealism is still there, and, if revived, could still do something to change the direction of British politics. The question is whether it is too late and whether the tide has been missed through internal squabbles, confused values and naked ambition for centralized power. If so, people may well turn to the unknown factor of the Liberal-Social Democratic Alliance with its promise of a new way forward based on co-operation rather than confrontation and building community afresh from the grass roots. But the danger is that it may turn out to be the soft centre of British politics, predominantly middle-class, supported by those who do not want anything changed and wish to be left undisturbed. Alternatively, it could be the spearhead of a radical reforming movement: radical in the sense of getting to the roots of our social malaise.

Faced with the three major possibilities, Christians have to ask which of them offers the best promise of radical change, of replacing the values of acquisitive self-seeking for the values of mutual responsibility in the service of the community. It will have become obvious where I stand. The Conservative Party seems to me to be set in precisely the opposite direction to that in which we ought to be heading. The Labour Party still retains some of its idealism, but has lost its way. The Alliance at least offers hope of a constructive way forward. But all the parties reflect the self-seeking attitudes which they themselves have done so much to encourage. None is as yet sufficiently radical to grasp that nettle. Therefore, Christians have to take the political options as they are presented, recognizing the relativity of each of the alternatives, but identifying with what seems to be more nearly in tune with the values enshrined in the gospel.

That is why it makes sense to say that the church should stand above party politics; not for the prudential reason that identification with any one party would cause divisions within parishes and congregations, but because the relativity and ambiguity of all political programmes entail a legitimate variety of responses. This is the overwhelming case against the establishment of a Christian political party. Where that has been tried on the continent of Europe, it has proved to be socially divisive and has limited the prophetic calling of the church to challenge all the political options. No serious argument for a Christian party has been advanced in Britain, and we may be thankful for that. It is far better for Christians to face the complexity of the problems presented by the alternatives on offer and not to be misled into believing that there is a Christian option which will provide a way of escape from identification with the struggles of a pluralist and transitional society.

As long as the party game is played according to the present rules, we have to abide by them and do the best we can. But that is not to say that the rules cannot and should not be changed. This is arguably the major question with which we are confronted in so far as we seek to revitalize our democratic institutions. Nobody can gainsay the fact that the system of 'first past the post' at elections has progressively eroded representative government. For many years the party in power has been voted into office only by a minority of the electorate, and those millions who have refused to support either the Conservatives or the Socialists have been grossly under-represented. Moreover, in any constituency votes for all the candidates who lose are wasted in terms of any degree of representation they might have in the councils of the nation: an outcome which affects Tory and Labour voters alike in the many safe seats where they are in a permanent minority. Hence it is not surprising that the campaign for electoral reform and the introduction of some form of proportional representation has been gaining ground across the whole political spectrum, while the opinion polls consistently show an overwhelming majority in favour of change in this direction.

The principal arguments against it are that it would inhibit strong and decisive government and that it would weaken the ties between a member of parliament and his constituents. These are presented as purely administrative considerations, and when in 1980 the British Council of Churches endorsed the report of a working party on Electoral Reform which advocated proportional representation, Hugo Young, the political editor of *The Sunday Times* reacted by saying that it made him want to reach for his Missal! It is appropriate, he said, that the churches should speak out on racial discrimination and unemployment where moral questions are clearly at stake, but not on technical questions such as this.

Whether he had read the report I do not know. If he had, he would have discovered that the members of the working party had spent a great deal of time discussing the value assumptions underlying technical considerations and had concluded that the more the technical argument is pressed, the more important it is to penetrate behind it to discover what is being concealed and particularly the ends that are being taken for granted. The case for proportional representation rests on the need to establish trust on the part of the people in those elected to office and to control unbridled use of power by ensuring the maximum spread of responsibility within the legislature. Both of these objectives are grounded in beliefs about the nature of man and the structuring of relationships within society which are an inevitable Christian concern.

The BCC report concentrates on the first, identifying what many would call the alienation of the electorate from the democratic process as evidence of sloth, engendered by the belief that votes do not really count. If support is to be secured for the legislature at either national or local levels, it must be seen to be fully representative of those entitled to vote; otherwise it will increasingly be felt to reflect only a sectional interest seeking to impose its will on the rest of the population. Every vote should count as far as possible. While the members of the Working Party acknowledged that proportional representation would not be a cure for political apathy, and did not want to make any extravagant claims for it, they did believe that it could be a significant step towards correcting the drift away from any sense of commitment to the political process.

The report was also critical of the argument that 'first past the post' ensures strong and decisive government. This seems to me to be the real hub of the matter. Is such government self-evidently desirable? The experience of the post-war years would appear to indicate that it is not. The spectacle of a government supported by a minority of the electorate seeking to impose its will on the nation, only to be succeeded by the opposition doing the same, spending much of its energy trying to unscramble the work of the previous administration, has been in no small measure responsible for our national malaise. It has created an atmosphere of instability in which long-term industrial and social planning has become almost impossible, strikingly evident in the confusions of policy in the direction of our nationalized industries. One chairman after another has resigned in frustration at the vacillations of ministerial interference, often dictated by changing ideological pressures. The best government is one that provides a stable context within which the affairs of the nation may be conducted.

Proportional representation would go a long way to curtail the unbridled exercise of power and ensure the maximum degree of consent for any legislation. In the end such consent is necessary for the legislation to be effective, certainly if the understanding support of the people at large is to be secured. The largest party in Parliament or on the council would not then be able to ride rough-shod over everyone else; it would have to compromise in the interests of securing wider agreement. That is undoubtedly an uncomfortable prospect for those politicians who want to get their own way at all costs; but it also reveals the danger they are to themselves as well as to everyone else. Unbridled power is dangerous; distributed power is a safeguard against its abuse. The

Christian understanding of human nature underscores that analysis.

Once the arguments for strong government have been discounted, the case for retaining the present electoral system in Britain becomes a flimsy, if not a purely self-interested one. Members of Parliament are often heard to say that proportional representation would destroy the relationship to their constituents because it would involve multi-member constituencies or party lists covering widely dispersed geographical areas. Certainly the freedom to approach a member of Parliament about personal problems is an important feature of our democratic system, and the surgeries which are regularly held by politicians of all parties throughout the country are a valuable safety-valve as well as a direct means of redressing grievances. It is also important that local councillors as well as members of Parliament should have specialized knowledge of the problems and possibilities of a relatively small community or section of the population. But it is not beyond the bounds of ingenuity to preserve this under any electoral system. There is nothing to stop politicians agreeing amongst themselves how to divide up this responsibility. From the point of view of the elector it does not really matter whom he approaches as long as he knows to whom he can go.

When the arguments against any change in the system are taken apart, the true objection is revealed as the reluctance of those concerned to give up the game as it is now played. For one thing, many of the players would lose their places in the team, and that would be bad for them, though not necessarily for anyone else. But they have become used to the game and enjoy playing it according to the rules which dictate whether you win or lose. To turn politics into a co-operative enterprise for the welfare of the nation is to ask for a radical change of attitude. Does that mean that we have outworn the usefulness of the party system as such? Certainly it has its defects viewed from the standpoint of the way in which it inhibits the participation of ordinary citizens in the democratic process. For example, the selection of candidates is generally in the hands of a small caucus of activists from which even the supporters of the party concerned are often excluded. But even if the selection procedures were altered to allow more people to have a say, the average voter would still be faced with a limited choice.

I do not see how this can be avoided. It is impossible for everyone to have detailed knowledge about every possible candidate. Even when independents stand at local elections, they are personally well-known only to a comparatively few people. It is the party label – even the label of independent – that generally identifies them. Only where a very small number of people are concerned can the choice of a person solely in his or her own right become decisive. The party system is the best we have for providing electors with a genuine choice between alternatives. It may not be perfect, but we have to make it work as well as we can. And that is why we cannot remain content with the game as it is now played. It excludes too many people from the degree of participation in the political process which it is possible for them to exercise.

There is a wide measure of agreement amongst Christians that this is so, reflected in the readiness of so many representatives of the various churches to adopt the report of the BCC's working party. When this degree of unanimity is reached, it should carry a good deal of weight, signalling that the game is over except for the final whistle. A rearguard action may be sustained for some time, but the outcome looks inevitable.

The practice of party politics may have fallen into disrepute, but suspicion centres even more on what is referred to as the Establishment. Asked to define its meaning anyone could produce a catalogue of estates of the realm: the Royal Family, the Court, the House of Lords, the Church of England, the Judiciary, the Civil Service, the Armed Services, the Police, the Bank of England, the Confederation of British Industry, the Newspaper Proprietors Association, the British Broadcasting Corporation, the Independent Television Authority and the list of 'the good and the great' from which selection is made for public office. The word 'Establishment' suggests something that is immovable and impervious to change. Whether or not this is a justifiable description of the institutions so categorized, the suspicion is widespread that together they constitute a network of power outside public control, turning what we claim to be democracy into a charade.

A number of questions are raised by this fashionable attack on the 'Establishment'. Is the criticism of its very existence misdirected? Is it sufficiently accountable to public opinion? What should be its proper relation to an elected parliament? Does it stand in need of reform?

The first thing to say is that much of the criticism stems from deep-seated jealousy: the resentment of those excluded from positions of influence against those who hold them. In the sense that the Establishment is taken to comprise all those estates of the realm which by their very nature are administered by comparatively few people, there is always the tendency for it to be attacked by those who secretly wish that they had the power and influence which others have got. Much of the high-sounding, moralistic condemnation of privilege cloaks a belief that the wrong people enjoy it, not that it is wrong in itself. Some kind of establishment is necessary for the conduct of the nation's affairs, and the dismantling of what we have would require its replacement by something else of the same kind. There is as much of an establishment in the Soviet Union as in the United States, Britain or any other country. Whether we like it or not, it is necessarily the prerogative of the few. To resent this is to camouflage envy and covetousness which are rooted in the self-centredness that is a denial of Christian values.

However, the serious criticism of the Establishment is directed against the way in which it is recruited and the sources from which it is drawn. The Victorian attack on privilege was launched against the restricted aristocratic and land-owning circles which dominated the state. Merit and ability, it was argued, should determine who were appointed to positions of responsibility, not birth or patronage. The battle has been waged ever since and, although great progress has been made, there are many who believe that it has yet to be decisively won. Common to all the institutions making up the Establishment is that they are not open to election by popular vote nor are they directly subject to the House of Commons. Some would argue that they should be, or at least that they should be more effectively, under democratic control.

The House of Lords is the principal target. Many argue that it is an outmoded bastion of inherited privilege and should be abolished. Others are in favour of its reform by turning it into a second elected chamber. This raises the general question whether popular election always secures the best result. Would we then want to go on to get rid of the monarchy and elect the judiciary after the American pattern? Few would be inclined to advocate such proposals. The Crown is more firmly established in popular estimation than any other estate of the realm. Setting a standard of public service which few in the Establishment emulate, though all recognize as normative, the monarchy is seen as a focus of national unity and a stabilizing influence unaffected by the fluctuating tides of political opportunism. Amidst all the glamour and excitement of Presidential elections, the American people have a wistful attraction to the British Royal Family. It is above party politics and does not have to seek power or influence. That is its strength. Again, if we want an impartial judiciary, free of corruption, we are much more likely to have it if it does not depend on courting popular favour, as happens in the United States.

Elections, therefore, have their disadvantages. They do not ensure or even make likely that those best qualified for office will be successful. Popular franchise, extended to every public institution, would be a recipe for incompetence. A healthy society requires a balance between those elected to direct the nation's affairs and those who are appointed to responsibility on the basis of merit. If the distribution of powers is to be advocated as the result of a Christian understanding of human nature, then there is not only a strong case for institutions governed by those specially qualified to do so to check and be checked by an elected House of Commons, but also for a variety of such institutions which counter-balance one another. To bring them all under the direct control of Parliament would be to centralize power in too few hands; a state of affairs exacerbated as long as the two-party game continues to be played according to the prevailing rules.

This is the case against an elected second chamber, though its preservation on that basis would be much preferable to its abolition. There is something sinister about the campaign to get rid of it altogether; for it is a step towards totalitarianism: the belief that government, however appointed, should be all-powerful. The existence of a second chamber with limited power, designed to scrutinize legislation laid before the House of Commons and to call for reconsideration of measures on which there may well be more to be said, is a safeguard against the passing of hastily conceived and ill-considered bills. For that to be acceptable, the

House of Lords has to be seen to be composed of those with a wide variety of expertise and representing many different points of view.

To a greater degree than in the past, that is how it is today, assisted by the creation of life peerages. But there is a good deal of scope for reform. Too much depends on the hereditary principle and prime-ministerial patronage. A policy of nomination from what I have called the other estates of the realm would open the way to a more broadly based second chamber. The number of Anglican bishops could be reduced and their contribution balanced by representatives of the Roman Catholics, Church of Scotland and the Free Churches. Places could be found for nominees of the CBI, the TUC, the Universities, the Voluntary Social Services, the Overseas Aid Agencies, the Local Authorities, the Ethnic Communities, to mention only a few. The object should be not to secure a proportionate balance between the political parties in the House of Commons, but to produce a cross-bench chamber of those with a particular contribution to make: a corrective to those whose absolute commitment to a political party tends to make them blind to the merits of anything that conflicts with their partisan programme.

The main objection to the British Establishment has always been the sources from which its personnel has been recruited. In the nineteenth century, as I have already said, the Liberal reformers attacked its domination by the aristocratic and landowning interests which for long had effectively excluded the rising middle classes with their leadership in industry, business and the professions. More recently criticism has been directed against the old-boy network: the preponderance of recruits from the independent schools and Oxbridge. Almost every discussion about the composition of the civil service, the judiciary and other estates of the realm has tended to produce a statistical analysis of the schools and universities from which they come. In so far as this represents a protest against the exclusion of any on the basis of merit it is fully justified. But the argument is often pressed too far, concealing ingrained jealousies and prejudices. In recent years Oxford and Cambridge colleges have been increasingly concerned to ensure the selection of those students whom they believe to be best fitted for the kind of education they provide, irrespective of the schools from which they come. If candidates from these or other institutions turn out to be the ablest in competition based on merit, that is an argument in favour of maintaining the high standards of excellence, not for discrimination against them. Statistics are often used in a misleading way. The predominance of the public schools and Oxbridge does not necessarily imply prejudice in favour of those who come from a particular social background; in so far as this continues to be so, as it undoubtedly was in the past, it should be strenuously resisted. However, to put this into reverse and claim that a candidate should be given special consideration because he or she was educated at a comprehensive school and one of the polytechnics is equally discriminatory. Ability and promise should be the criteria, not social background.

That said, there is still room for radical improvement in educational opportunities and selection procedures, about which I shall have more to say in a later chapter. In particular, the British Civil Service suffers from the narrow academic preparation which most of its promising recruits have had. One of the principal defects is the lack of industrial and business experience in its senior administrative grades compared, for example, with their counterparts in France. There, those destined for government service and industry are educated together in the Grandes Écoles and particularly in L'École Nationale d'Administration, while transfers of senior personnel from one to the other are reasonably common.[4] Since an establishment is necessary in a modern complex society, it should be both diversified and open: open to the ablest people irrespective of social background, open to the challenge of fresh ideas, and open to the stimulus of those with differing experience.

But I return to the crucial importance of democratic influence and control. It would be a misreading of the preceding paragraphs to conclude that I am advocating a modern form of the élitism which Plato so powerfully defended in the *The Republic*. As I argued in the previous chapter, Christians cannot accord to themselves or anyone else, however able or experienced, a monopoly of wisdom or freedom from the danger of corruption. Moreover, essential to the Christian understanding of human nature is the belief that everyone has the potentiality of making a contribution to the body politic. Amongst the most unlettered there is often found a depth of wisdom far beyond the reach of the most sophisticated. The establishment, therefore, requires counter-checks within itself, the direction of those elected to Parliament, and on the part of both sensitivity to the aspirations of ordinary people. In the end, the values cherished by men and women at large will determine the kind of society we will have. Changes in our democratic structures or the replacement of one party in government for another will achieve little of lasting importance without radical alteration in the attitudes of ordinary people. Ultimate values are at stake and these lie at the heart of the Christian gospel.

4

Freedom and Equality

Underlying the party political debate is the conflict between the values of freedom and equality. Conflict it is, because, if either is elevated to become the final standard for social values, all that stems from the other is placed in jeopardy. It is impossible to press the claims of freedom in absolute terms without disadvantage to other people. Conversely, the demand for equality can be purchased only at the price of considerable inroads into personal liberty. This is the dilemma which has produced the polarization between the political right and left, leading to increasingly deep divisions in British society. Has a choice to be made between freedom and equality as the touchstone of public policy, or are there values which transcend both and enable us to see a way of preserving what is essential in each of them without the one contradicting the other?

Answering this question entails a critical analysis of popular notions of what both freedom and equality are taken to imply. To begin with the former, if we are to get our thinking straight, nothing is more important than to penetrate behind the superficial slogans so frequently bandied about when politicians and statesmen talk about 'the free society' or 'the free world'. For many who live in the countries of the West the words have a hollow ring. They find themselves trapped in an economic and social system in which the choices open to them are extremely limited. Their destiny, as I have already said, seems to be in the hands of others and they feel helpless in the face of the bureaucracies and the managements which decide what they ought to do and how they ought to live.

At the moment of writing, a dispute has erupted at British Leyland's Cowley works about the imposed withdrawal of a three-minute washing-up time at the end of each shift. To the outside observer it may have seemed to be a trivial issue for bringing the production lines to a halt. But those who have had experience of working on the shop floor in the car industry and in similar highly automated plants know the degree to which the operative feels he is an extension of the machine. Admittedly, Cowley had a bad strike record and the management was determined to make the business competitive. But people can be pushed around only so far; the moment comes when they feel that they are no longer being treated as human beings with a life of their own. That is what obviously underlay the dispute to which I have referred. The immediate cause may have seemed to be trivial; the sense of being treated like slaves, whatever the financial rewards, ran deep. Men and women cannot be compensated by money for what they feel to be a loss of human dignity.

This is but one passing example of the limitations to the claim that we live in a free society which should be the envy of the whole world. We justifiably cherish our freedom of speech and assembly, the adult franchise, the opportunity to change the party in government, the safeguards against intrusion into our privacy (though developments in information technology and data processing have recently made these more problematical), and the relative impartiality of our legal system with the right to challenge injustice in the courts. But we should be chary of claiming too much for our democratic system. Under it one man's freedom can still be another man's subjugation.

If subjugation is too strong a word to apply to most situations in which people find themselves, there can be no doubt that the exercise of freedom on the part of some leads to disadvantage and even exploitation on the part of others. This is an inevitable concomitant of the free enterprise system and the attempt to extend an unregulated market economy, of which I shall have more to say in the next chapter. Hence the invocation of the egalitarian principle by the Labour Party and the trade unions to defend the freedom of those who are subject to exploitation, though it is a striking fact that a fairer distribution of financial rewards has tended to be the prime objective rather than the achievement of more equitable responsibility for taking decisions affecting everyday living. However, the latter has not been lacking, as the illustration from the Cowley dispute makes plain.

Nevertheless, it is in the sphere of everyday human relationships that the unchecked exercise of personal freedom can be most destructive, and every society has had to take measures to restrict it and keep it under control. This is most obvious in the passing of laws to deal with murder, the infliction of grievous bodily harm and the theft of property. Extended to legislation against slander and libel, racial discrimination, hazards to health, pollution of the environment, violations of planning policy, to take only a few of the possible examples, the question arises where government interference in the freedom of individuals should begin and where it should end. No clear understanding of any underlying principle appears to lie behind the decisions made by public authorities, who seem to have based legislation on the uncertain judgment of what people at large are prepared to tolerate.

Examples of the confusion in which we find ourselves can be drawn from the growth of permissiveness, particularly in our sexual mores. Nobody who walks through the streets of Soho, sees the proliferation of sex shops in all our big cities, takes account of the sale of pornographic literature, or scans the pages of *The Sun* and the erotic magazines can seriously doubt that a vast industry has grown, almost unchecked, designed to make as much money as possible out of the degradation of human beings. To suggest any kind of censorship provokes not only fierce opposition from those who stand to gain from their sleazy enterprises but the specious argument that nobody has any business to stop people getting what they want. Yet acquiescence in this state of affairs is profoundly illogical if we are not prepared to extend the same permissiveness into almost every field of government restraint on the liberty of the individual. Why should it be justifiable to prevent anyone doing what he likes with his own house whatever the views of the planning authority, if he is quite free to exploit the bodies of young girls? Does this mean that things matter more than people? Is the difference that girls are to be regarded as sex objects, to be discarded like empty cans, whereas houses last for many years? To put the questions in this provocative way shows the confusion into which we have sunk in our understanding of the proper exercise of freedom and its restraint.

A not so obvious example of the dilemma of the so-called free society is the claims of the media to publish and broadcast anything that journalists or programme presenters wish to do. We rightly cherish the freedom of the press and the liberty to express opinions however unpopular. We have seen how totalitarian governments can manipulate the media to their own advantage and suppress all forms of criticism. Yet the power in the hands of a very few people in this country to decide what should be printed and what values should inform television and broadcasting is enormous. People's reputations are destroyed and their privacy ruthlessly invaded to secure sensational stories which can be marketed for profit. But when those responsible are criticized, there is all too often an arrogant reaction, voiced in the claim that nobody should interfere with the free expression of views. As one newspaper editor said in my hearing some time ago, there were liable to be 'outraged screams' on the part of some of his staff at any suggestion that they should not be allowed to publish anything they liked to write. *Their* freedom should be protected, however rough-shod they were to ride over the freedom of others to seek any redress.

Freedom is, therefore, a problematic value. It is rooted in the inalienable right of every individual to develop his own distinctive personality without being arbitrarily prevented from doing so by the activities of anybody else. But we run into difficulties whenever one man's or woman's freedom overrides that of other people; and that is in danger of happening all the time. However, the attempt to redress the balance by invoking the principle of equality produces its own set of problems. Grounded in conviction about the ultimate worth of every human being, egalitarianism is seen as the basis for countering the unbridled exercise of freedom and as the criterion for the proper ordering of society.

Once again confusion enters into the picture. People are different in capacity, background, tastes and aspirations. When equality is advocated, are we in danger of ending up with a grey uniformity in which no one counts as a person with his own distinctive individuality? The cult of egalitarianism was superbly caricatured by W. S. Gilbert in *The Gondoliers* where Don Alhambra sings of the king who

> . . . wished all men as rich as he,
> so to the top of every tree
> promoted everybody.

But when everybody was either a Lord Chancellor, a Bishop, an Ambassador, a Prime Minister, a Field Marshal or a party leader, then the conclusion was obvious:

> When everyone is somebodee,
> Then no one's anybody.

The trouble is that equality is a mathematical notion, attributable to things and not to people. Before we know where we are, human beings are computerized, classified, reduced to numbers in a card index. And it is a short move from that to treating them as things to be slotted into some pigeon-hole, the helpless victims of bureaucratic organization. This is no fanciful nightmare; we see ominous signs of what can so easily happen all around us.

Nobody who wants to uphold the principle of equality as a social value ever intends that it should be understood in a purely quantitative sense, but it is a slippery notion. While the distinctive value of every person is ultimately at stake, the consequences to be drawn from that are both quantitative and qualitative. Gross disparities of income and to some extent of opportunity can be quantified; differences in natural endowments and aspirations cannot be so assessed. No amount of social engineering can or should turn a surgeon into a bricklayer or vice versa; people are not interchangeable. The bricklayer has a distinctive value as a bricklayer, and the surgeon as a surgeon. Egalitarianism can so easily be corrupted by envy and the idea of levelling, which begins as the wholly laudable intention of raising the standard of living of those who are deprived and oppressed, and then turns into a campaign for drab uniformity, the results of which are strikingly apparent to those visiting countries under communist rule.

Theoretically, the equalization of incomes is quantifiable and therefore, in principle, attainable, but hardly anybody believes it to be politically practicable, and the majority would probably think it unfair on the ground that greater responsibility and harder work deserve a larger financial reward. That is, of course, debatable, especially when the consideration is introduced that the lowest paid jobs often involve unpleasant drudgery, whereas many of the highest paid afford a considerable degree of interest and pleasure to those fortunate enough to have them. But the discussion at this level is largely academic. The attempt to enforce equal pay right across the board would run into such resistance that no government of any complexion would be able to carry it into effect. That is as true of countries under Communist rule as of those in any other part of the world. Nevertheless, while the equalization of incomes is recognized to be impracticable, an overwhelming case can be made out against the gross disparities between the very rich and the very poor. It is obviously wrong that many of our fellow citizens live at a barely subsistence level, while others are paid huge salaries at the head of large industries, in the higher reaches of the professions and in the entertainment world. Nobody's contribution to society is so unique or so onerous as to justify the sort of differences which at present obtain. If the answer is that the market dictates what anyone can earn, we are entitled to reply, 'So much the worse for the market; intervention to redress the balance is morally justifiable and may well be politically acceptable.' But this is not equality. If we work to move in the direction indicated, we need some other criterion to help us preserve what is intended without absolutizing a problematic ideal.

Even greater difficulties arise if we aim at equality of opportunity; for this, unlike money, cannot be precisely quantified. The attempt is made to do so, for example, in respect of jobs, education and accessibility to health care. Taking the first of these, nobody can seriously claim that anyone should be hired or given an appointment without regard to his or her qualifications. That would be a lottery resulting in square pegs in round holes. What is at stake is unfair discrimination on the grounds of sex, race or social background, though the latter may sometimes, perhaps often, disqualify a certain person for doing a particular job. Someone coming from a home where books are never read, where bingo, the horses, the dogs and the football pools are the main topics of conversation, is inevitably disadvantaged in seeking employment where imagination and initiative are required.

To counteract such disadvantages, many have looked to the introduction of comprehensive schools for the provision of equal opportunity. But this has proved to be more intractable than the most ardent advocates of the system have often been prepared to admit. Quite apart from differences in homes and neighbourhoods between one catchment area and another, schools differ according to the qualities of the heads and the teachers, and within the comprehensive school as at present organized selection takes place according to the estimated ability of children to pass examinations. I shall have more to say about this in a later chapter. But the point I am wanting to make here is that equal opportunity in education is highly problematical simply because of the inherent differences between children's capacity to respond to a given educational environment. It is the human factor which defeats social engineering.

Medical care is different because, by definition, patients inevitably place themselves in the hands of doctors and nurses. Their freedom of choice is limited to whom they may happen to go. They can decide on their general practitioner and, in case of need, can often express a preference for a certain consultant. The National Health Service was designed to make such provision accessible to everyone, irrespective of their ability to pay. In some areas, as in Galloway where I live, this works exceedingly well and there is virtually no demand for the introduction of private medicine. The latter arises only where the provision is inadequate, where there are long waiting queues for hospital treatment or where the number of patients on a doctor's list is so large that people feel that they cannot get sufficient personal attention. But these defects are remediable. Of course, no system, however well organized, can guarantee equal standards of treatment simply because some doctors and hospitals are better than others. This is the point at which the standard of egalitarianism inevitably breaks down; it is once again the human factor which calls it in question.

All the same, there are values inherent in the principles of both freedom and equality which need to be preserved and somehow reconciled to one another. One way of beginning to see how this may be done is to return to a redefinition of freedom. If it is understood simply as the absence of restraint and the ability to do what you want, disastrous social consequences follow. That is not how the leading Liberals of the late nineteenth century interpreted what they called 'the voluntary principle'. They sought to define it in a positive sense as 'the liberation of the powers of all men equally for contribution to the common good'.[1] In other words, a distinction was being drawn between freedom *from* restraint and freedom *for* the fulfilment of life. This was illustrated some years ago by the novelist, George A. Birmingham in a parable related to the 'Four Freedoms' which Franklin D. Roosevelt enunciated in his Annual Message to Congress, delivered on 6 January 1941 as the guiding principles for a future world order: freedom from want, freedom from fear, freedom of speech, and freedom of worship. The bear in his cage at the zoo, said Birmingham, enjoys all the four freedoms. He has freedom from want: he has as much as he needs to eat. He has freedom from fear: nobody is going to attack him. He has freedom of speech: he can growl to his heart's content. He has freedom of worship: that is if he knows how to do so. But he isn't free to be a bear, to enjoy his natural habitat in the Rocky Mountains. So men and women are not truly free until they discover their essential humanity in contributing to the common good.

This is an important distinction. But Victorian Liberalism in its reliance on the voluntary principle was unable to deal with the mounting social problem of the century's closing decades. What it did was too little and too late. The leaders of the working class and the trade unions had become disillusioned with the Liberal Party, believing that only by taking power into their own hands were the necessary structural changes going to be effected. Hence the Labour Party was formed, securing its first elected members of Parliament in Keir Hardie and John Burns, and replacing the Liberals as the main opposition to the Conservatives after the signing of the armistice in 1918. From then on egalitarianism replaced voluntarism as the guiding principle for radical social change.

As we survey the scene today, there has been a strange reversion to mid-Victorian attitudes amongst people at large. This has been encouraged by the resurgence of right-wing politics in the Conservative Party, but it has also infiltrated the whole of the Labour movement. Freedom is widely interpreted, as we have seen, to be the pursuit of your own interests even to the extent of doing just what you want to do, unimpeded by anybody else and regardless of the consequences for others. Those on the right and left of the political spectrum would doubtless protest that this is not what they are intending and they would point to the policies which they are seeking to implement as evidence of their concern for the welfare of the whole nation. This is not to be denied. But it does not alter the fact that attitudes have been inculcated in the population at large which run counter to anything which makes for social cohesion. The prevailing idea of freedom comes dangerously near to undermining the best that was enshrined in the voluntary principle of the Victorians and reverting to the free-for-all of the jungle. Despite the high-sounding and sincere intentions of the politicians, what ultimately matters is the attitude of ordinary people. In the end their values will dictate the direction in which society is heading. As long as the touchstone is 'You have to look after number one,' disintegration of society and disaster lie ahead.

What should the Christian response be to this confusion of values? Clearly it is important to preserve the essentials in the ideals of equality and freedom, provided that a way can be found of reconciling them with each other. That means taking the positive content of the voluntary principle as far as it will go. According to the Bible, man isn't free until he discovers what he is meant to be: the servant of God and his fellow men. This releases him from slavery to his own selfish desires and bondage to the secular standards of society: what St Paul calls slavery to sin and subjection to the principalities and powers. That is not the exchange of one tyrannical rule for another, as some have suggested. It is deliverance from all that prevents growth into full humanity and submission to the persuasive powers of divine love: willing obedience to him 'whose service,' in the words of the Book of Common Prayer, 'is perfect freedom'.

Nevertheless, that has to be balanced with respect for the dignity of every other human being and the contribution he or she has to make to the development of true community. This is what is really essential in the idea of equality. It means going beyond the Victorian understanding of the voluntary principle by recognizing that it is not the prerogative of the privileged to bestow benefits on the less fortunate. They in their turn need the ministry of the disadvantaged to show them the poverty of their own privilege and the obstacles to their own salvation through the perpetuation of the structures of injustice. According to the New Testament, it is in the faces of the poor, the outcasts and the disadvantaged that Christ is to be seen.

Let not this be misunderstood. I am not saying that in the purpose of God gross inequality should be preserved to shame the rich and the powerful. Rather, I am claiming that from the Christian point of view we should begin by reversing the roles taken for granted in the Victorian espousal of the voluntary principle. It is the potential contribution to society of those who are at present disadvantaged which holds the key to overcoming our class divisiveness and opening the doors to more genuine human community. Therefore, I believe that the idea of mutual responsibility comes nearest to the insights of the New Testament: the expression of the covenant between God and man as a covenant of mutual responsibility between those who are alike the recipients of his grace. The sacrament of the eucharist – the new covenant sealed in Christ's blood – wherein bread and wine are shared is the sign of God's purpose for the whole of humanity. This takes up the essentials of freedom and equality, transcending them by placing them in a wider perspective.

At first sight this may seem like taking off into the theological stratosphere. It is not. The notion of mutual responsibility is as intelligible as freedom or equality and may prove to be more acceptable as a criterion for political action in so far as it avoids the pitfalls inherent in absolutizing the values I have identified as problematic. However, the objection may well be raised that the exercise of mutual responsibility presupposes a motivation of moral behaviour which is not amenable to legislation and therefore to the implementation of political policy.

A good deal of confusion arises at this point. It is obvious that you cannot compel people by law to change their attitudes. That can be done only by persuasion. However, it is equally true that no society can have any coherence without the general acceptance of certain values and their translation into political policy and ultimately legislation. The question is what those values should be and how far legislation can be taken to put them into effect.

Some years ago the issue was brought into the sharpest focus by a controversy between the eminent judge, Lord Devlin, and the professor of jurisprudence, H. L. A. Hart. The former had argued in a lecture on 'The Enforcement of Morals' at the British Academy that there was no escape from the conclusion that the law was designed to enforce moral standards, while his critic maintained that the state was entitled to go no further than to prescribe a framework intended to prevent anyone actually harming anybody else. Within those limits everybody should be free to adopt his own moral standards whatsoever they might happen to be. It was unfortunate that the discussion centred on sexual mores, where the case for the freedom of private judgment could be most plausibly argued. Of course, if Lord Devlin's contention had proved to be unanswerable, the whole framework of Professor Hart would have been called in question. Conversely, to have challenged the framework would not necessarily have opened the door to legislation in what many would regard as interference in their private lives. It would, however, have raised the more important question of how far the state should go in promoting the common good. It was unfortunate that concentration on sexual behaviour prevented the larger question from being adequately discussed.

As Professor Basil Mitchell points out in his survey of the debate,[2] the protagonists shared a larger measure of fundamental agreement than on first impressions might have seemed to be the case. Both held that certain values had to be embodied in the laws of the land for society to have any coherence. They differed on how far state interference in private life needed to go. However, the weakness of Professor Hart's case lay not in his particular arguments against Lord Devlin's views about the propriety of legislation in the fields of sexual and marital conduct, but in his belief that a free society depended on restricting legislation to the prevention of harm being done to any member of it. This was tantamount to a reversion to the Liberalism of the late nineteenth century, and it can be argued that no government in this country of any complexion has subsequently been prepared to accept such a negative role. Even the Thatcher administration, which at the time of writing has been trying to put the clock back and speak of the reinstatement of Victorian values, has not gone so far as to abandon the role of the state in promoting the common good. It is committed to putting in reverse the expansion of government provision which has characterized all administrations since the end of the war, not to abandoning it altogether.

The question before the country is how far people are prepared to support collective action at both national and local levels not simply to counter the consequences of private self-interest being allowed to run rampant, but to promote co-operative efforts to achieve the general welfare. This is partly a question of general principle, partly of how far that principle is to be put into effect. For Christians, as I have already argued, I believe the basic choice is clear: co-operation is fundamental, and in our deeply divided society that is what we should seek to uphold. But unless prevailing attitudes change – and it is unrealistic to suppose they will change rapidly – there are limitations on what can effectively be done. Coercion through legislation is counter-productive unless it is tempered by persuasion and undergirded by widespread popular support.

That is a lesson which the governments of Eastern Europe will gradually have to learn. One of the most hopeful signs for the future is the resistance of the Polish people to the imposition of martial law. In the short term General Jaruzelski may have succeeded in clamping down the lid on popular aspirations, but he has done so only at the cost of further alienating his fellow-countrymen from the Communist government of which he is the head. That cannot last. No country can prosper, no administration be indefinitely sustained, against the combined resistance of a resentful and determined population. The Polish people in their overwhelming allegiance to the Roman Catholic Church draw on spiritual resources which are ultimately far more powerful and enduring than the brittle might of ruthless oppression.

In this country there has been little deep reflection on the Polish phenomenon. The rise of Solidarity and its resistance to every attempt to suppress it have been watched with admiration, but also with a kind of fatalism: it has too easily been assumed that nothing can be effective against overwhelming military force. We seem to have lost faith in the power of the human spirit, let alone its reinforcement by the Spirit of God. History testifies to the transitoriness of tyrannical government and the abiding strength of spiritual values, evidenced even in the short run by the survival and growth of the church in the Soviet Union and the People's Republic of China. However, one is left wondering whether the same resilience would manifest itself in the countries of the Western world, where freedom from oppressive government seems to have been accompanied by lack of concern for ultimate values. I vividly recall the shock experienced by a group of Canadian students when they were told by a young minister from Moscow studying theology in their own university that, while he was not a Communist and rejected the ideology of Marxism, he would not choose to live in their prosperous city because, he said, 'You seem to have no social purpose.'

This is not an argument for the benefits of living under an oppressive régime; it is rather a reminder that we can lose our sense of direction and relapse into a privatized world of self-interest when there are no constraints upon us to look to any standards of social value other than the promotion of our own advantage. We have not reached that sorry state yet. There are reserves of moral energy in the British people which can be called upon in a time of crisis, as happened, for instance, when Nazi barbarianism was threatening the advent of a new Dark Age. But we cannot trade on that remaining so, and there are ominous signs of a self-interested cancer eating at the soul of the nation. We need to lift our sights by establishing mutual responsibility and co-operation in service to one another as our supreme social values. That cannot be legislated. No government can enforce it. It depends on a change of attitude amongst the mass of ordinary people enabling the government of the day to adopt policies which embody such values and provide a context within which this expression can be encouraged.

5

A Humane Economy

The story is told that at the end of the Second World War the distinguished economist, John Meynard Keynes, was questioning a Treasury official, who told him that the country couldn't afford to rebuild the bomb-damaged sites of London.

'Haven't you got the bricks?' asked Keynes.
'Oh yes, we've plenty of them.'
'You haven't got the steel, the wood, the fittings, the machinery?'
'No, that's not the problem.'
'You haven't got the labour?'
'Oh, there are plenty of people coming out of the forces.'
'I see what you must mean. You haven't the architects?'
'Of course not. The real problem is that we haven't got the money.'

The point that Keynes was making is obvious: money in itself is valueless. Its value is to be measured only in what it represents in land, raw materials, machinery, products and services. The paradox which Keynes was high-lighting is the absurdity of arguing that we cannot afford to do what is needed when all the resources are available for doing it, simply because we cannot manipulate the currency. This is reminiscent of an incident reported some time ago in the press when a civil servant shook his head in perplexity during a committee which had decided that a certain project was feasible. 'You can't do it', he said. 'We couldn't manage the paper work!'

Nevertheless, when there is sufficient conviction that something needs to be done, the money is found. Nobody argued that Britain could not afford to go to war in 1939 because there wasn't enough money available. Nor did the government consider that financial cost was a crucial factor in deciding whether to send the Task Force to the South Atlantic in 1982, and the huge expenditure on defending the Falklands as an island fortress was accepted, at least by the Conservative party, without a demur. The specious explanation is to claim that in both cases there was a clear priority in what had to be done and therefore money had to be used for these purposes rather than for any other. It is true that resources in men and equipment were used for waging war rather than for producing consumer goods or social services. But if the Argentinians had not invaded the islands, would that have made any substantial difference to employment here at home? However we answer the question, what we are talking about is not the availability of money, but the way in which our resources are used. Money reflects that. It is not a scarce commodity which has to be rationed and therefore deployed in one way rather than another. It is a convenient symbol to facilitate the exchange of goods and services. When the latter become depressed and are in short supply, the currency is inflated. An upturn in the real economy makes money cheaper, provided that salaries and wages are not recklessly increased. The charge against monetarist policies is that they deal with the symptom rather than the disease. They seek to stimulate economic activity by manipulating the symbols rather than by tackling the problems at their roots.

For far too long we have been mystified by money. Many people spend their lives trying to make as much of it as possible and not a few are occupied with playing the financial markets. But the exchange of money in itself produces nothing of value, and when hoarded it is completely useless. Yet people spend their lives pursuing it for its own sake. The folly of this was exposed long ago in the Book of Ecclesiastes: 'The man who has money can never have enough, and the man who is in love with great wealth enjoys no return from it. . . When riches multiply, so do those who live off them; and what advantage has the owner, except to look at them?' (6.10–11, NEB). Only when put to work does money have any real significance, and that entirely depends on the demand for goods and services and their availability. Therefore, if we want to get to grips with what the economy really is, we have to penetrate the smoke screen; we have to ask what kind of economy we want: what real resources are available, what sort of goods and services we require and how are they to be distributed.

It takes an effort of the imagination to put the questions in this way because the general public has so long been conditioned to think of money as a commodity and the ultimately valuable commodity at that. This popular misconception is compounded by the professional economists and those who depend on their calculations and predictions in so far as they deal with what can be precisely quantified. Money readily lends itself to this purpose. Put a price on something, whether it be an article sold in the shops or a service rendered, and you can calculate its value, but that is computing the exchange rate, not the inherent value of what is on offer. The problem for the economist is that the latter is not quantifiable. You cannot measure in figures an unrecognized work of art or a service that is freely given.

This means that when the economy is discussed, only that which is bought and sold is taken into account; much that is genuinely productive is necessarily ignored because it will not fit into the criteria for assessment. The management of a household and raising a family are the most obvious examples of what is excluded from the gross national product as viewed from the standpoint of the economist. But there is much more besides. All voluntary activity, whether organized or not, contributes to the welfare of the community. As long as the accumulation of money or figures in a ledger are taken to be the criterion of wealth, it is impossible to raise radical questions about the economy.

Another common misconception which inhibits clarity of thinking is the widespread assumption that manufacturing industry is the only source for producing wealth, that the service industries are parasites upon it, and that public expenditure is entirely subsidized by it. This general impression becomes established in the public consciousness by the superficial generalizations of politicians and their reflection in the media. Of course, it would be nonsense to contend that the manufacture of commodities does not itself produce wealth when that is defined as what people need to procure or use. Moreover, if we are to be able to purchase goods from abroad, selling what is manufactured in Britain, together with invisible exports like insurance, is measured in the maintenance of a balance of payments. But the emphasis on manufacturing industry as the real source of wealth reflects an excessively materialistic view of human aspirations. We do need food, clothing, shelter and a whole range of manufactured products to sustain a reasonable standard of living, but we need much else besides, and it is by no means obvious that the volume of goods produced sustains those services which may be privately or publicly provided rather than the other way about. The two are intertwined and mutually dependent, supporting one another rather than the one being parasitic on the other. It is just as inaccurate to say that public expenditure on social services is dependent on the profitability of manufacturing industry as to maintain the reverse.

The popular misconception is due to the valuation placed on material possessions which are tangible and to some extent quantifiable as against the benefit of services rendered. Why, for example, should it be assumed that the manufacture of a car by British Leyland produces wealth, while the completion of a successful surgical operation does not? The latter is likely to be far more important to the patient than his ability to own the latest model which comes off the production line. If we are to achieve a balanced economy, still more if it is to be a humane one in the sense of serving truly human interests, we have to cut away the undergrowth of the prevailing mythology which prevents us facing the real issues.

This leads to a still more uncomfortable question which politicians of all parties have for the most part been unwilling or unable to ask. Has the time come to challenge the objective of indefinite economic growth defined as the unlimited expansion of the gross national product? As we have seen, this is commonly understood to be the manufacture of an increasing number and variety of commodities irrespective of their inherent value. Over the past few years there has been a growing movement of those who have warned against the wastage of natural resources and the pollution of the environment which so often accompanies it. The rise of the Green Party in the Federal Republic of Germany has been the most notable example of organized political pressure in this direction. But it is reflected in all the countries of the Western world, not merely in the fringe ecology parties, but in the growing sensitivity of governments and political parties of every complexion to environmental hazards. So far, however, a largely rearguard action has been fought against the most blatant encroachments on precious natural reserves and their prostitution for quick profits at the expense of other amenities. Those responsible for manufacturing industry exploit the resources at their command as far as they are able to do so, restricted only by overwhelming public pressure. It is taken for granted that as much as possible should be produced within limits which should be drawn as widely as they can be. Even those firms most sensitive to environmental considerations assume that expansion is an obvious benefit, not only to their management, employees and shareholders, but to the nation at large.

It is this assumption which deserves the most rigorous scrutiny. Is it self-evident that increasing industrial production, irrespective of what is produced, is a rational objective, or does it lie at the root of the economic malaise of Western society? Some years ago I was travelling in a restaurant car on the railroad to New York. My companion turned out to be one of the barons of the steel industry, and during lunch he regaled me with a description of the five or six houses he owned in different parts of the United States, including a weekend cottage to which he invited his business associates several times a year, and which was looked after by a couple who owned their own property in the Deep South on the strength of the salary he paid them. Following this disquisition on the benefits of wealth, he began to talk about the material prosperity that the future promised to every American citizen. It was now common for a working man to own a home, a car, a television set, a refrigerator, a washing machine, and all the modern domestic appliances; and this would soon be the good fortune of everyone. 'What then?,' I asked. 'Oh, everyone will have a larger home, a larger car (more than one), a larger television set, a larger refrigerator, a larger washing machine. . . !'

The bizarre picture this presents of indefinite economic growth is rendered somewhat more plausible by diverting attention to the variety, rather than quantity, of possible provision through the development of human inventiveness, and the manifest need to improve the lot of those who are at present deprived of standard consumer goods and still more of the millions who live in abject poverty, often below subsistence level. But that is to ask questions about what should be produced and how it should be distributed. It is not a prescription for economic growth as such; and it is this which needs to be challenged, as an end in itself, if we are to get to grips with genuine human needs.

Here we come to the crunch of the matter. What kind of economy do we want to have and on what principles is it to be based? For Christians this is an inescapable question if we are to take the will of God for human society with any seriousness and see how the quality of life can be improved for everyone. At this point it is worth pausing to put aside premature considerations which prevent many people taking a cool, hard look at the question. Quite apart from the diversion to which I referred in the previous paragraph, there is a tendency to jump to the feared consequences of any radical reappraisal of economic objectives: the loss of personal freedom to make one's own way in the world; the threat to established jobs; the dead hand of corporate planning. The party political debate too quickly takes over the argument, compounded by the prejudices and fears of the average voter about the way in which he or she is likely to be affected by the choice of economic priorities. Before becoming entangled in questions of the means to achieve certain ends, we must first become clear about the ends we wish to attain.

From the Christian point of view we have to aim at a society in which basic human needs are fully met. At the minimum this covers adequate food and clothing, a house or apartment in which to live and some facility for recreation. To many people in Britain it has come as a shock to realize that several millions of our fellow-citizens do not enjoy even these basic amenities. In a survey conducted in the summer of 1983 by Market and Opinion Research International the results showed that 2.9 million could not afford a roast joint or meat chop once a week; 4.3 million do not live in a damp-free home; 3.25 million have no adequate heating and 1.1 million are without a bath; 3.4 million entirely depend on second-hand clothes and 2.9 million do not possess a warm coat; 9.7 million cannot afford a week's holiday away and 2.2 million are deprived of the opportunity of a Christmas celebration. Those suffering this degree of deprivation were, not surprisingly, found to be predominantly among single-parent families and the unemployed.

That is only the tip of the iceberg. The squalor and overcrowding in inner-city areas, the drabness and lack of social amenities on many housing estates contribute to a wider context of deprivation than the survey discloses; and many people would want to add a list of requirements for a basic standard of living not covered by those already mentioned such as a television set, a washing machine, a refrigerator and toys for the children. That would extend the range of the poverty trap a great deal further.

Tackling this blight on British society should surely be the first priority of economic policy. A nation that does not do so is scarcely worth defending, and that needs impressing upon those in government who set the defence of the realm above everything else. It is nonsense to say that we cannot afford to do it or that it can be done only gradually and piece-meal. One of the most striking results of the MORI survey was the readiness evinced from ordinary people to have taxes increased to deal with the problem, and that applied to 79% of Conservative voters whose party was pledged to reduce taxation as an economic priority! That is the first step towards facing our responsibilities to the underdeveloped nations, to those millions who live on the verge of starvation and are deprived of all the basic necessities for existence. But we are unlikely to take this really seriously until we have come to terms with poverty in our own midst. The time has come to put this in the forefront of political policy, and Christians have a duty to be in the vanguard of those demanding it.

However, with rising expectations of material prosperity it is impossible to draw a sharp line between genuine needs and extravagant or artificially contrived wants. Nevertheless, it is feasible to make a broad distinction and to bring under critical scrutiny the most obvious lack of balance in the Western economies. This has been a constant theme in the writings of the American economist, John Kenneth Galbraith, which have had an extraordinarily wide circulation amongst the reading public, but have hardly made any impact on political policy at least as far as the challenge to unlimited growth in manufactured products is concerned; for those engaged in industry, both in management and on the shop floor, simply do not want to listen. Yet he successfully punctures the illusion that the market is wholly responsible for demand and consumer choice. If this were so, he asks, why do millions of dollars and pounds have to be spent on advertising new products? It is not simply to inform, but to persuade people that they need to buy what otherwise they would never have thought of wanting. So all kinds of throw-away products and ingeniously packaged commodities flood the market which do not really improve the standard of living of those who buy them or enhance its quality. Set over against this private wastage is what Galbraith rightly castigates as public squalor: the pollution of the environment, the decay of urban areas, the run-down of social services of all kinds and the poverty trap.

We have to ask whether our huge resources of ingenuity, materials and manpower are being misdirected, channelled into wasteful and even destructive enterprises.

The most obvious example is the expanding arms industry. If the vast expenditure of effort in inventing and manufacturing weapons were devoted to the elimination of world poverty and the improvement of the quality of life of all peoples, the human scene would be totally transformed. That would undoubtedly match the aspirations of the mass of ordinary men and women, but as long as we have not found ways of curbing the ambitions of power-hungry politicians and the fears on which they thrive, it is unrealistic to suppose that the arms trade can be drastically cut back or the resources which it voraciously consumes be redirected. However, what we can do is to expose the danger of the one feeding the other. There are vested interests in stoking the fires of fear, distrust and ambition in order to expand a world-wide industry which affords rich profits to a few in disregard of the spread of human misery and suffering entailed thereby. To some extent, even to a large extent, the manufacture and export of armaments is governed by considerations of foreign policy. Whether we agree with that policy or not, this is at least a defensible criterion, because it can be argued that the public interest is at stake. However, economic arguments for expansion or even for the maintenance of existing levels are another matter; and these can so insidiously influence what actually is done. The aim should be not to expand, but to cut back as far as that is consistent with the defence of the realm. In saying this, I am not begging the question whether any particular defence or foreign policy is soundly grounded. That is reserved for discussion in the final chapter. Here my concern is with the economics of the arms trade: the proliferation of wastage for destructive purposes.

When we turn to other aspects of the real economy, it is evident that radical changes are inexorably taking place. Old established industries, such as steel, shipbuilding and textiles, are in rapid decline due either to lack of demand or world competition. When there is a glut of products, plant will be dismantled, firms go out of business and jobs will be lost. The trade unions will naturally fight this every inch of the way; for their *raison d'être* is to defend the interests of their members and to secure their means of livelihood. But the most far-sighted of their leaders know full well that they are battling against an inevitable tide which rolls relentlessly onwards, and the best that they can hope to do is to cushion the shock until new forms of employment become available. This has permeated remarkably quickly to the rank and file and largely explains why a Conservative administration which had presided over a staggering increase in the number of unemp'oyed was returned to power in the general election of 1983; a kind of fatalism had taken root in large sections of the work force. Moreover, it had become widely recognized that whatever party achieved office, it would inevitably face the same problems; the hardship might be mitigated; the number of unemployed be reduced; but the shake-out in British industry was unavoidable. Where demand is decreasing and order-books stand empty, there is no hope of shoring up the old edifice.

Before attempting to look to the future to see what kind of economy is sustainable and how human needs and aspirations can be met as we move towards the dawn of another century, we have to ask whether the full measure of the changes taking place is being realistically faced. We know that certain industries have no future and that others, particularly in the fields of electronics and information technology, have bright prospects. But we are still bitten by the bug of economic growth for its own sake; we are producing many things which we do not need while neglecting other work crying out to be done.

The car industry is a good example, commonly assumed to be

one of the main indicators of economic performance. A rise in the number of vehicles manufactured and sold is seen as a sign that the country is on the road to recovery; a slump in sales signals the reverse. It is taken for granted that this is an industry which should be encouraged to expand without limit. New models are designed to supersede the old, turned out with largely cosmetic changes to titillate the fancy through massive advertising campaigns, intended to go out of fashion and be consigned to the scrap heap after a few years, to be replaced by even larger quantities in greater variety than before. Does this make any kind of economic sense? The prospect of clogging the roads with a volume of traffic that brings everything to a virtual standstill beggars the imagination. We have almost come to that already in the centres of our major cities, and it stands to reason that the congestion will spread to the countryside if the sky is the limit for production. As a temporary expedient the demand has grown for a massive expansion of the road network, covering valuable land with miles of tarmac, destroying natural amenities and making towns and villages the victims of the voracious passion to get from one place to another by one's own private vehicle. And there is a physical limit to that as well. Add to these considerations the toll on life and limb which mounts every year from this most dangerous form of transport. We may well ask whether we have taken leave of our senses.

In the meanwhile the railways have gone into decline. Thousands of miles of track were axed by Lord Beeching; still more are threatened; rolling stock has been allowed to become antiquated; services have deteriorated; and the whole concept of an integrated public transport system has been shelved by successive administrations.

The response to this is that that is what people in general want. But is it? Even if it were, we cannot have it in the form of an indefinite extension of the road along which we are travelling; the whole system would grind to a halt and end in a nightmare. Nevertheless, it is too readily taken for granted that more and more people need a car or at least ought to want one or even two or three! For many it has become a necessity because public transport is not available. Bus services in many districts are either infrequent or non-existent. Railway stations have been closed, tracks torn up and lines discontinued. But it is rapidly ceasing to be a pleasure or even a convenience to travel by car; many prefer to make their way by public transport where it is possible; and many more would do so if it were made attractive. In the cities the car is beginning to become obsolete. With parking problems and congestion on the roads, growing numbers, particularly amongst the young, are taking to bicycles. It is now the quickest and cheapest way of getting around parts of London. Even those who could afford the most expensive type of private car sometimes find it more convenient to travel by taxi. Some years ago a cab driver in Washington DC told his passenger that a millionaire in the city had laid up his Cadillac and decided to use a cab as frequently as he would use his own automobile. His savings were enormous and he was spared the strain of driving. This was doubtless exceptional at the time, but it made sense. If public transport was more flexible and was imaginatively planned, with the introduction of mini-buses on suburban routes and collective taxis for several passengers at a time on major thoroughfares, the existing bus, underground and commuter services could be supplemented, and the private car become a thing of the past in all our major cities.

We do not face up to realities because of vested interests, lulled into acquiescence by skilful and massive advertising. The motoring organizations and the road hauliers constitute a powerful political lobby. The manufacturers and the trade unions would fiercely resist any suggestion that their industry should be curtailed; though in passing it is worth noting that its expansion would not provide more jobs or even sustain the present level of employment; automation and robots are fast taking over the manufacture of cars and trucks. Only those taking the short view of how to preserve the jobs at present held can have any reason to resist a radical review of the industry. Most of them face the prospect of a diminishing work-force even on an expansionist programme.

I have taken this controversial example of a major industry which is commonly regarded as a barometer of economic performance to suggest that, if the needs of society are adopted as the criterion, even the sacred cows are not exempt from questioning. I am not arguing that we should cease to produce cars or trucks or stop building and improving our roads. That would be foolish iconoclasm. However, I am maintaining that the goal of indefinite expansion has to be abandoned and that retrenchment is even desirable in the interests of a more sensible transport system. That is the kind of conclusion to which we have had to come in the case of other industries, like the production of steel, and it opens the way to a reconsideration of the whole of our economy.

In particular, attention may begin to be redirected towards those things which most obviously need to be done. The sewers and waterways are long overdue for modernization. Tens of thousands of new houses need to be built and antiquated ones replaced or refurbished. Large areas of the inner cities require reconstruction and public amenities for leisure and recreation expanded. The health and social services call out for major improvements, and, if we are to provide for the changing patterns of living as we approach the twenty-first century, a massive enlargement and diversification of the whole educational system is probably going to become the main social priority. Of this I shall have more to say in the next two chapters. Here I simply make the point that there is no lack of work that needs to be done if the general quality of life for all our people is to be improved.

Immediately the question arises 'Who is to pay for it?' Where is the money to come from? This presupposes that the basic problem is a financial one and that economics, defined in monetarist terms, is the determinant of what can be achieved. Is it not rather a political question; political interpreted in the widest possible sense as what people want their society to be, what are their priorities, where and how they are prepared for the resources of materials and man-power to be deployed? These are political questions. Or, to put it differently, financial and economic considerations are subservient to political goals. We have too long been mesmerized into thinking that finance dictates economics and in turn dictates politics. The reverse is the case. The economy is a human creation, dependent upon human decisions. We talk about it as if it had a life and momentum of its own about which we can do nothing. That is the fundamental error leading us to imagine that the availability of money determines everything we do, whereas the decisions taken about priorities for the use of manpower and resources ultimately dictate the money supply.

To ask, therefore, where the money is coming from to pay for what needs to be done is to pose the wrong question. Rather we should be directing our attention to the kind of economy we want. Are we looking for a boom in consumer spending or for an improvement in the amenities which enhance the possibility of a qualitatively better life for everyone? This is partly a matter of balance between what people expect to consume and possess on the one hand and, on the other, the facilities they require for health, education, leisure and the enjoyment of their environment. But it is also a matter of priorities when the balance becomes grossly distorted. It does so whenever consumption threatens to destroy the social fabric on which civilized life depends. To put it in an extreme form, do we want to go on adding to the pile of junk and waste at the expense of the pollution of the environment, the decay of our cities and the decimation of our public services?

Focussing attention on these questions does not automatically lead us to adopt a particular party political stance. Whether state provision or private enterprise is the way to achieve the desired results or whether some combination of the two is preferable remains open for debate. Here I am concerned with ends, not with means. So much confusion arises from a failure to distinguish between them; and this happens whenever a particular political method of attaining certain ends becomes an end in itself. This so easily becomes the trap into which the zealous advocates of both privatization and government provision tend to fall. It is not obvious, for example, that steps towards an integrated transport system are likely to be taken through extending the facilities for competitive enterprise; perhaps it can be achieved only by state planning. On the other hand, it is not necessarily the case that the only method of securing improved health care for everyone is to require the ministry in Whitehall to provide it. Recent proposals for ancillary services in hospitals to be contracted out to private operators may or may not be a more efficient way of providing for catering and laundry; and there is an argument in favour of using voluntary nursing homes at public expense to care for geriatric patients and the chronically sick, freeing hospital beds for those needing minor operations who are at present on long waiting lists. I am not here entering into the merits or otherwise of these proposals. They are simply illustrations of legitimate arguments about means to secure the objective of comprehensive health care.

The basic question, then, is about the kind of economy we seek to achieve. From the standpoint of Christian values this should clearly be one which ensures the maximum co-operation in providing everyone with the fullest opportunity both to contribute to and to enjoy the fruits of man's inventiveness. It should be measured not by the quantity of what is produced, but by the quality of life in community. The welfare of people should take precedence over the valuation of things which should be regarded as instrumental to human needs and not objects to be pursued for their own sake. In short, it should be a humane economy in which mutual responsibility is shared for the benefit of all.

That is an ideal goal. But is it what people want? Is it even what most Christians want? It is easy to give lip service to it, but when practical steps are suggested to move in this kind of direction the commitment to selfish ends becomes apparent and the pursuit of material possessions seems to over-ride all other considerations. This is the measure of human sin in which we all share and the denial of which is sheer self-deception. The recognition that that is so can lead to cynicism and acquiescence in the competitive rat race. But most people retain at least a residuum of social responsibility even if it extends no further than to their family and circle of friends. The most common characteristic is a muddle between supposed self-interest and concern for the welfare of other people.

This is reflected in the policies and programmes of all the political parties, and it could hardly be otherwise if they were to have any chance of capturing public support. There may be a few on the fringe of the right wing who are simply concerned to secure the freedom of a minority to exploit the rest of the community to their own material advantage. But the Conservative party as a whole is clearly committed to the public welfare. Otherwise the Tories would be advocating the total destruction of the health and social services. When their opponents castigate them for trying to roll back the frontiers of the state and claim that they intend the destruction of all public welfare provision or that they would retain it only to the extent that it keeps the mass of the population quiescent, this is an obvious distortion of what is really intended. Exaggeration is ultimately counter-productive in terms of carrying conviction. Nor is it true that, apart from a tiny minority on the extreme left wing, those who advocate the growth of public expenditure and the expansion of the role of the state have no concern for the freedom of the individual and his responsibility for making a contribution to society. Indeed, those on the political left often seem to be as much committed to self-advancement as the most die-hard proponents of free enterprise. The fact is that when it comes to considering ends rather than means there is a great deal of confusion across the whole political spectrum, reflecting the tension in the minds of ordinary people between their own materialistic ambitions and their sense of responsibility for the common interest.

A recurring theme of this book has been the importance of being realistic, of facing the human situation as it really is, and at the same time keeping ideal goals in view. Practical politics is the business of relating the one to the other and moving, however painstakingly and whatever the frustrations, towards the desired end. But no effective progress can be made without clarity about objectives, and, if a more humane society is our aim, if we want to achieve a more balanced economy which really enhances the quality of our national life, then we must ask some fundamental questions about the goals we are currently pursuing. For the remainder of this chapter I propose to concentrate on some of the changes in the attitudes of ordinary people that will be required if we are to escape from our present confusion.

First of all, we need to decide whether the improvement of our economic infrastructure – sewers, waterways, roads, railways, utilities and the natural environment – and our communal services – police, fire protection, education, health, care of the aged, the handicapped and the socially inadequate – (and these are examples, not an exhaustive list) – are just as important to all of us as the production of consumer goods and more important than the indefinite increase of their quantity and variety. As I have already made plain, we do need to manufacture products for export as well as the home market. But the infrastructure and services are just as vital to the well-being of everybody. What, then, does it mean to say that we cannot afford them at their present level, still less bend all our energies to improving them? Is it that the materials and people are not available? Or is it that their employment would divert resources from manufacturing industry?

That will not stand up to examination at a time when there are qualified teachers, nurses, social workers and tens of thousands of technicians and manual workers unable to find jobs. Of course, the tragic problem of mass unemployment cannot be immediately solved by an expansion of the services which are now being reduced. Many people are in the wrong place, made redundant from industries which can no longer survive; many are not equipped for the jobs that need to be done. But where there are people available, what sense does it make not to use them? The answer is that it would cost money to pay them. Here we come to the crunch. What does it mean to say that money cannot be found? It means that the bulk of citizens want to retain the power of purchasing consumer goods whether they do so or not. It is fundamentally a question of choice and demand. The money is there in people's salaries and wage packets, in their savings accounts, bank balances and investments: all of it so much paper except in terms of purchasing power. The trouble is that they are reluctant to have it used for the purposes I have outlined. Hence the resistance to rates and taxes which have come to be regarded almost as raids on the private purse, to be avoided by any means, legitimate or otherwise. In other words, the money supply is not the problem. What is at stake is the relative value set on consumer products with the potentiality of acquiring them and the services on which everybody depends for a civilized life.

The cynic will be inclined to say that, human nature being what it is, attachment to individual purchasing power will always prevail. But that is not wholly borne out by the facts. If it were, no resources would be diverted from satisfying consumer interests. Imagine the public outcry if any government were to propose the total abolition of the educational, health and social services, let alone the infrastructure of utilities and the maintenance of protective agencies. We have come a long way in this century in supporting and extending this sort of provision. However, the question is now whether we are in danger of slipping backwards instead of building on what has so far been achieved. It is all a matter of public attitudes. We can stop the drift and turn the tide if we are prepared to do so; and that means a growing number of people recognizing that unbridled consumerism is not an acceptable goal and that the provision of a better infrastructure and range of services is now the social priority.

One of the principal difficulties in securing this change of outlook is the remoteness most people feel from the control of government expenditure. Rates and taxes are paid into a vast pool, the disbursement of which is settled in the recesses of Whitehall or County Hall. The sheer size of the amounts involved and the complexity of government administration leave the average citizen bewildered, prone to the suspicion that he is being milked for sustaining a cumbersome bureaucracy which spends much of its time generating mountains of paper. Caricature though this is, it is the sort of image that has lodged itself deeply into the public consciousness. The suspicion is further compounded by the uncriticized notion that the government has a bottomless purse at its disposal which makes taxation a kind of confidence trick by which the citizen is exploited to feed a predatory animal. Hence tax avoidance becomes a legitimate game to play: a contest against a powerful adversary whose defeat is something of a triumph for common sense.

In so far as this represents popular attitudes, it is irrational and known to be irrational when anyone thinks about it. But people are generally governed by feelings, not by reason; and there can be no doubt that there is a widespread feeling of alienation from the whole process of government. It is difficult to feel involved in the provision of many of the services we take for granted and on which we depend for the conduct of our daily lives. When a woman goes into a shop to buy a loaf of bread or a battery for a transistor she is conscious of paying for what she gets. She pays, too, for services like hairdressing and dry-cleaning. She does not feel the same about having the policeman on the beat, the fire station round the corner and the local school. They are provided by someone else: the council, the government, the collective 'they'. And yet 'they' are her agents in ensuring that she has what she demands and for which she, with many others, has actually paid.

Part of the difference lies in the fact that, when a woman buys anything off the shelf, it is a matter of choice whether she does so or not. She can choose whether to spend the money on a loaf of bread or a pint of milk; there is no personal decision involved in whether the policeman is on the beat or in a panda car or for that matter whether he is there at all. And yet there would be an outcry if nobody appeared when the house was burgled; the difference is not as great as it is felt to be.

If there is to be any change in attitudes to social provision, we have to recognize that much has to be done to make ordinary people feel that they have a responsibility for the services on which they depend. One major step in this direction is to press for the maximum devolution of powers from Whitehall to the regions and the local authorities. But we have to go further. Local councils are also felt to be remote and insensitive bureaucracies. There are many things that they alone can do, but there has been a tendency in many places for councillors and their officials to arrogate to themselves the exclusive responsibility for community welfare, suspicious of voluntary organizations and private initiatives in meeting human needs; they are sometimes seen as an implied criticism of the council for not doing its job properly. Happily that is ceasing to be the case, particularly when public authorities are faced with severe financial restraints. The thrust of the argument, however, is that where people can combine together for the benefit of their community they should be encouraged to do so.

Another important step towards changing attitudes is the way in which public officials approach their own job. Too often they are seen as petty autocrats, dispensing largesse to a subservient public. It is a common complaint that the clerk behind the counter at the Town Hall, the housing department, the rating and social security offices treats anyone who comes as a potential nuisance, seeking favours which have to be reluctantly granted. And that is where most people meet officialdom and that is where they derive their image of insensitive bureaucracy. Of course, there are many exceptions. But it would be revealing to ask the clerk behind the counter who he or she thinks is their employer. The instinctive response would be the boss upstairs. It would be a startling suggestion that the harrassed housewife or the bewildered form-filler is actually the person who employs them and to whom they are ultimately accountable. The whole idea of public service has become debased and needs reinstating if the alienation to which I have referred is to be corrected and prevailing attitudes changed.

Fresh thinking is required about accountability for social

provision. The political debate is largely concerned in ideological terms with the relative merits of government management and private enterprise. It is much more important to ask how social needs may most effectively be met whether by government action or private initiative and how either can be made more responsive to the interests of the average citizen.

So far I have indicated the need for change in the attitudes of ordinary people towards a balance between personal consumption and social provision and their sense of responsibility for the latter. Now I want to go on to face the much more difficult problem of pay and prices which has bedevilled every British government over the past twenty years or more. The story is a familiar one. As goods in the shops became more expensive through the increased cost of raw materials imported from abroad, dramatically accelerated by the sudden quadrupling of the price of oil, so higher wages and salaries were demanded to keep pace in purchasing power, fuelling an inexorable spiral as the cost of labour added to the price of goods. The result was a rapid retreat from reality. Those who succeeded in keeping abreast of inflation were able to conceal from themselves that the real cost of merchandise had actually risen. Many more, not only those belonging to powerful trade unions, but those in management and the professions, found themselves better off as increases in earnings outpaced the price index. The sirens of alarm sounded by industrialists, economists and government spokesmen went largely unheeded by those who were cushioned at least for the time being against the effects of what was taking place. But for those who were unable to protect themselves, especially those living on fixed incomes, rapid inflation was disastrous. Moreover, the low-paid, the pensioners and those unable to work increasingly felt the pinch as percentage increases in the money they received added comparatively little to the amount they had at their disposal. The prices to be paid were the same for everybody, but a 10% increase on a high salary or even on £100 per week was very different from that on £50 or under. The rich were getting richer and the poor poorer as inflation took its toll.

Then the chickens began to come home to roost for many of those who at first had been lulled into a sense of security by the increases in their salary cheques and pay packets. Businesses started to collapse, factories were closed, redundancies became the order of the day as one after another firms found themselves unable to sell their products at competitive prices, and unemployment reached a level which bid to outstrip that experienced in the pre-war years of depression. The main brunt fell on employees, though management was by no means exempt.

The Conservative government under Margaret Thatcher has not surprisingly been blamed for what has taken place; for it has presided over the most serious escalation of the problem. Whether or not it has taken the right steps for dealing with the crisis is a matter of debate. I certainly would not wish to defend either the policies it has adopted or its general approach. But at least it has tried to get to grips with inflation and has had a measure of success in doing so. My main objection, as I have already said, is that it has been trying to deal with the symptoms instead of combatting the disease. And that has been the trouble not only with its predecessors but with the public at large. We are all to blame for our failure to face reality over many years, and so find ourselves confronted with a restructuring of the real economy, unprepared to do so. One government after another has ducked the issue largely because the electorate as a whole has been content to live in cloud-cuckoo-land and was believed to be unwilling to face uncomfortable facts.

Whatever government had been in power, the shake-out of British industry was inevitable. Patterns of world trade have been changing. Some of the old-established industries have become obsolete. Competition to sell goods abroad has become more intense. Merchandise must be marketed of a quality and at a price for which people at home and abroad are prepared to pay. That means that we cannot afford to pay salaries and wages which do not reflect the real value of what is being produced. We have, therefore, to rid ourselves of the idea that we can increase wealth by increasing the amount of money at our disposal. Our problem is that we have come to believe that everyone is entitled to receive more money every year and that to get richer in money terms is the natural and reasonable goal at which everyone should be expected to aim. The only result of pursuing such an illusion is diversion from attention to the real economy of the production of goods and services and the growingly unfair distribution of the means whereby those goods and services may be procured. The time has come to halt the automatic increases in salaries and wages and concentrate on their more equitable distribution amongst the whole population.

Finally, we need a new attitude towards work. Escalating unemployment in the industrialized countries has caught us unprepared to face the inevitable consequences of changing patterns of world trade, the rapid advance of technological invention and necessity of conserving scarce resources. It is no good crying over split milk or bewailing the lost opportunities of recent years. We have now to look to the future and see what has to be done to secure not only a livelihood for all our people, but a satisfying way of life, particularly for those who have become victims of structural upheaval.

The loss of many repetitive manual jobs is not in itself to be deplored. Indeed it is to be welcomed. The dehumanizing labour of the monotonous production line is soul-destroying, stifling self-development and reducing men and women to cogs in a machine. Whenever working people are described as hands or are treated as tools in an industrial process, they are being debased; and that has been the lot of so many over the past century or more. Their replacement by automated machinery and robots is in itself a liberation, provided a way can be found for those made redundant to be creatively employed. But to be thrown on the dole queue and regarded as society's rejects is even more dehumanizing; for those engaged in repetitive piece-work at least have some sense of being wanted, even though they may feel undervalued as human beings and have no interest in what they are doing.

If, then, we are to find a creative way forward, we have to begin by changing our attitudes to hard labour. There is no virtue in working for its own sake, irrespective of what is in fact done. This so-called Protestant ethic has taken deep root in the public consciousness, infecting even those whose employment is recognized by themselves and others as involving initiative and responsibility. The 'workaholic' is to be found in every walk of life. In so far as toil in itself is regarded as a virtue, we are seeing things out of perspective. The promise of Jesus was that he came to bring life and life more abundant. That is the true human destiny: living, not penal servitude with hard labour. We should not have to live to work, but work to live. Therefore, the loss of repetitive and often useless toil should be welcomed in so far as it releases men and women for creative activity.

There lies the problem. Large numbers of people are unprepared for anything except routine manual labour and many others who have held executive or professional positions for which they are no longer required find themselves at a loss when they are debarred from the one thing they have been doing for so long. I shall have more to say about this in the next chapter when discussing education for living as a means of widening horizons and opening up fresh opportunities from childhood to old age. In the meantime we have to face the fact that tens of thousands of our people will be unable to find paid employment and many more will have to come to terms with part-time jobs or reduced working hours. Instead of regarding this as a recipe for enforced idleness, we must begin to see it as opening up fresh opportunities for creative activity which contributes to the welfare of the community as well as being self-fulfilling for those who engage in it. Managing a household, participating in a tenants' association, tending a garden, cultivating an allotment, pursuing hobbies, joining a sports club and a thousand and one other so-called leisure activities add more real wealth to the nation than standing in many a production line mechanically turning out by hand what can more efficiently be automated, not to speak of those commodities which would be better not produced anyway. We have to get away from the notion that only paid work creates wealth.

One way of changing attitudes and redirecting the emphasis to a more realistic future would be to guarantee to everyone a basic wage with family allowances, dropping the whole nomenclature of unemployment benefit and social security. This would go far to remove the stigma currently attached to the bewildering complex of hand-outs which millions of British subjects are entitled to receive and which are regarded by themselves and society in general as concessions to the unfortunate. To this basic wage anyone would be free to add whatever he could by paid employment, and the absurdity would be removed of penalizing people for doing even odd jobs by reducing benefits to which they would otherwise be entitled. In a just and caring society raising the basic wage would be seen as the compelling economic priority.

Of course, this whole approach is likely to be rejected by those who continue to believe that the only thing which really matters is to increase without limit the quantity of manufactured goods and that those who are most successful in doing so should reap the rewards in expanding incomes. It will be argued that mine is a prescription for economic decline, for the impoverishment of the whole nation by a failure to encourage the production of those things which we need for export and for improving our standard of living. Remove the incentive to work by paying higher and higher salaries and wages, and everyone will suffer. This results in the widespread assumption that monetary return is the only incentive for people to give of their best. That is not altogether true. Job satisfaction means far more to many than the amount they are paid. Not a few are prepared to accept lower salaries and wages for the sake of doing things they enjoy; and it is by no means obvious that highly paid executives would work less hard or less efficiently if their salaries were cut by £20,000 a year. Nor is it self-evident that the level of personal taxation in the upper brackets is a disincentive to production, though company taxation may seriously affect the profitability of a business. People may grumble about their levels of income and taxation, but that does not automatically mean that they would choose to give up their jobs or do them less efficiently.

All the same, maintaining the levels of production, expanding exports, starting new enterprises and filling the gaps in social provision are of crucial importance. We have to ensure that production keeps pace with the genuine requirements of the majority of the population and at the same time raises the standards of those who find it difficult to make ends meet. That also requires a changed attitude to paid employment on the part of those who are engaged in it. Instead of regarding it as a battlefield in which the strong drive the weak to the wall, we need to begin to see it as a co-operative enterprise for the welfare of the whole nation. Much is now being heard about partnership in industry and profit sharing, both necessary steps towards breaking down the barriers which bedevil the relationship between management and workers. But we shall make little progress without a radical change in the attitudes of all concerned by which service to the community replaces individual advancement as the motivating force behind every enterprise.

That may seem impossibly idealistic, given the ingrained selfishness of human nature. So it is, if we suppose that there can be a sudden and complete transformation of the attitudes we normally adopt and of the way in which we behave. But the opposite is fatalistic acquiescence in the law of the human jungle: every man for himself and the devil take the hindmost; human, because it is to sink far below the level of the animal kingdom. The fact is that for the most part we are a strange mixture of selfishness and altruism. At the fringes of society there are the saints and the hardened criminals; the former overwhelmingly motivated by altruism, but not quite, the latter overwhelmingly motivated by selfishness, but not quite. Most of us are a prey to mixed motives which we are rarely able to untangle with complete honesty, so often excusing our selfishness under a cloak of assumed altruism. That is reflected in our social, political and economic structures. Just as an individual begins to disintegrate when self-interest becomes dominant, so society starts to decay when the same principle becomes the touchstone for public policy. We have reached the point where we have to say that getting rich at other peoples' expense by regarding the acquisition of more and more money as a reasonable economic goal is totally unacceptable. Instead of the rich man being regarded as someone to emulate, we should be asking the uncomfortable question whether the possession of so much is a cause for shame when others possess so little. As Jesus said, 'A rich man will find it hard to enter the kingdom of heaven.'[1] We have to begin to take this warning seriously; for we have all been corrupted by the lust for money, from the millionaire to the low-paid worker dreaming of scooping a fortune from the pools. Admiration for the wealthy because they are wealthy sets a standard for everyone else which is a prescription for the disintegration of society. Its opposite, a caring and co-operative community, may be an ideal beyond human attainment, but at least it should be the pole star by which our economic policies are guided and governed.

There can be no doubt where Christians are impelled to take their stand about ultimate objectives, but more than anyone else they have reason to be aware of their own proneness to self-deception when it comes to working out the detailed policies to be adopted and of the hard kernel of self-interest which infects even the most altruistic intentions. Therein lies the problem with which we have to grapple: how to move in the direction of the goal while realistically facing the ambiguity of human nature. But without clarity regarding ends, without a change in public attitudes, towards which Christians have a contribution to make, there can be no movement away from cut-throat competition to a humane economy.

6

Education for Living

As I maintained in the previous chapter, we are living through a period of upheaval in the British economy and radical changes in the patterns of work and leisure. It is clear that there will be no return to full employment in the old manufacturing industries. Many believe that as technology advances, fewer jobs will be created and that they will be for the most part for highly trained, specialized personnel. The service industries will doubtless expand and new enterprises will be started. But it will be a long time before we have found a way of redeploying human resources in paid employment to give everyone the opportunity of a satisfying job; and with it will inevitably be greatly increased time for leisure activities through developments like work-sharing and reduction in the hours of the working week. Such a shake-up in British society is already taking place and its recognition is a commonplace, even if politicians will not admit it too openly in deference to the resistance of the public at large to facing uncomfortable change. Radical thinking about the future is inhibited by the all too human tendency to behave like the proverbial King Canute.

If society is undergoing radical change, it is imperative to ask how far our educational system is designed to prepare the young for living in it. Nobody who is prepared to face what is happening in our schools throughout the length and breadth of the land can be in any doubt that we are confronted with a deeply disturbing situation. Two recent surveys – one undertaken by a research team at the University of Edinburgh covering the reactions to their experience of school-leavers throughout Scotland and the other based upon interviews with a selection of young people between the ages of sixteen and twenty-three from Cornwall to the North of England[1] – reveal a striking consensus. Three impressions stand out. The first is that those interviewed did not believe that their schooling had prepared them for living in the world to which they had to adjust on leaving. The second is that they found school boring, being taught things in which they were not interested; and this applied to those who had succeeded in meeting examination requirements as well as those who were deemed to be incapable of making the grade and felt consigned to waste their time in useless attendance. The third impression is that they felt they had been treated as objects to be fitted into a slot, not as people who could be expected to act responsibly: the division between the authoritative 'them' and the subservient 'us' was deeply resented.

It is easy to dismiss these impressions by citing exceptions of which there are undoubtedly many or by saying that the young always react critically to their elders. There are many fine and imaginative teachers spread throughout our schools. But we would be simply burying our heads in the sand if we were to categorize the reactions of those interviewed in the two surveys as unrepresentative or to suppose that they do not reveal basic deficiencies in our general educational provision which we gloss over at our peril.

If we are to engage in radical thinking about new directions in educational policy, we have to be clear about the presuppositions from which we start. As Christians, we are committed to the belief that God values every individual child in his or her uniqueness and it his purpose that all should develop their full potentiality in relationship to other people. This means opening up the whole field of learning as a territory without limits to exploration or a fascinating voyage of discovery which does not end in the school classroom or university lecture theatre, but to which these should be a prelude: an introduction to growth in learning lasting a lifetime of widening horizons. That is not an unattainable ideal, as many can testify through their good fortune in coming under the influence of inspired teachers. And there is plenty of evidence of the desire to learn on the part of people of all ages in the growing use of public libraries and the demand for extra-mural and evening classes. The question to which we should be addressing ourselves is how far our educational system can be better adapted to this end.

This is surely the premise from which Christians ought to start; and, if we do so, we shall find that we have a surprising number of allies who do not necessarily make the same profession of faith as we do. Unhappily, we have to confess that the official organs of the churches have on the whole miserably failed to grapple with the basic question. They have been preoccupied with defending what is called religious education or the 'God-slot' in the curriculum, which, divorced from any meaningful relationship to everything else, is regarded by many children and teachers as an irrelevant waste of time. The late Professor Grenstead of Oxford once said that he was not so much concerned with the defence of the Christian Sunday as with the conquest of the pagan week. It is high time that we began to ask radical questions about educational policy as such, engaging in a debate which will have far-reaching consequences for the future shape of British society and to which the Christian understanding of God's purpose for human life is strikingly relevant.

We may profitably start by asking why the natural curiosity of a small child is so often stultified in the process of schooling, especially at the secondary level. Is it because, as we grow older, we become naturally less curious or is it because adults, parents and teachers alike, have stopped asking questions themselves, settling for limited horizons to which children are expected to conform? In so far as this is so, education will inevitably degenerate into the attempt to fit the young into a preconceived mould. There will be things they need to be taught to get a decent job, to pass examinations to secure better qualifications, to adapt to the expectations which parents have of them. School will be seen as a discipline for achieving certain limited goals and those who fail to match up to what is demanded of them become the rejects, compelled to work out their prescribed time to the age of sixteen by giving as little trouble as possible until they are thrown on to the labour market for unskilled jobs. Is it any wonder that the cross-section of school-leavers surveyed in the reports to which I have referred look back on their experience as boring and largely a waste of time?

Before anyone reacts adversely to what I have just said, let it be clearly understood that learning is not to be gained through idle and undirected curiosity. There is a heritage of acquired knowledge, wisdom and skills into which the young have to be initiated, and the teacher is rightly presumed to be equipped to do this. That does not need to be argued and can be taken as read. The question is whether the curiosity of the young is stimulated by the *way* in which the teacher approaches his or her task, whether the teacher is a learner capable of communicating his or her enthusiasm to the pupil and establishing a relationship which leads to mutual growth. That cannot be taken for granted, as the surveys quoted amply demonstrate.

It is on this that we need to concentrate, and it is simply not true that only the brightest children will respond to such an approach. That is belied by the many success stories in teaching the physically and mentally handicapped. Nor is it the case that disadvantaged youngsters from inner city areas are such problems that the only thing to do is to try to keep them in some kind of order and prevent them smashing up their environment. Any child or group of children treated as irredeemable failures is going to be confirmed in frustration and rebellion. Some of the most encouraging successes are to be seen where imaginative teachers have managed to win the confidence and enthusiasm of potentially wild and unruly children. The attitude and motivation of the teacher is absolutely crucial, and to this we shall return later.

Such teachers are scattered through the whole educational system, but unhappily they are a small minority and it is a matter of chance whether a boy or girl encounters one of them during his or her schooldays. The great majority of children find themselves confronted with those who have settled for the educational system as it is with its in-built constraints against learning and preconceived moulds into which the young have to be fitted. Even the most imaginative teachers cannot escape from this context, and much of what they try to do is constantly frustrated by the framework in which they have to work. The result is that for most children curiosity is progressively stifled. For some it is reawakened during a university course; for others it happens through the experience of life in their twenties or thereafter; for most it appears to lie dormant or else is never fully stimulated. How many older people who in later life have developed a widening range of interests look back on their schooldays as an experience from which they had to recover rather than the provision of an opportunity to embark on a fascinating voyage of exploration? As one who has enjoyed what most people would regard as a privileged education, on the whole I find myself in retrospect aligned with the young people whose views were reported in the surveys quoted.

If the basic purpose of education is to stimulate curiosity and awaken the desire for learning, we have to ask what are the main obstacles to this happening and in what ways our educational system needs to be and can be reformed. The place to start is with the attitudes and expectations of ordinary people; for in the end our institutions reflect the values which the population at large adopts. For the overwhelming majority, the purpose of education which I have outlined would be entirely strange. It is not that they have thought about it and rejected it; the trouble is that it has never occurred to them as a possible way of understanding what it is all about. The reason for this is not difficult to discern. Certain assumptions are taken for granted and never exposed to criticism. Basic to these is a sharp distinction between work and leisure, the former being regarded as a hard and unpleasant necessity while the latter provides the opportunity for enjoyment, the reward of engaging in wearisome toil. Although there are many people who derive pleasure from their work and more still who find their identification in the jobs for which they are paid, it does not alter the fact that the contrast holds, and those who enjoy their daily labour are regarded as lucky, gaining satisfaction from what is essentially an arduous business.

This attitude has taken deep root in the public consciousness, and, despite the derivation of 'school' from a Greek word meaning leisure, education is commonly regarded as falling within the category of work. In the pre-school group, in the kindergarten and to a diminishing extent at the primary level, learning is through play. The distinction at that stage does not arise, and children are expected to enjoy and do in fact enjoy the experience. But once a boy or girl reaches the age of about ten or eleven, expectations of parents and teachers alike begin to change. A future job now looms on the horizon; examinations have to be prepared for to secure the necessary paper qualifications; certain things have to be learnt and skills acquired to meet the tests. The school becomes work-oriented. While games and role-playing may still be part of the curriculum, the constraints of the ultimate objective of paid employment take over control, and with it the unexpressed assumption that boys and girls have to begin to become disciplined to the toil which will be their inevitable lot when they go out into the world. Education is expected to be a hard slog, doing things you don't want to do and are not even interested in doing because that is a preparation for what lies ahead. This is admittedly a sweeping generalization open to qualifications and exceptions. But the point I am trying to make is that there is an unarticulated feeling abroad that work is a kind of penal servitude bound up with monotonous drudgery which the young had better undergo as a discipline for what awaits them in later life. Children absorb this as part of the atmosphere in which they grow up and it comes to govern their expectations of what school is bound to be.

All the same, if this is the wrong way of looking at work, whether in the classroom or in the employment of the future, the fact remains that equipment for getting a job is of crucial importance to everyone, and most people take for granted that this is the purpose of the whole educational system. Certainly it is primarily directed to that end. The question we have to ask is whether the system as we know it is adequate to that objective, and more importantly, whether the objective itself is too narrowly conceived.

When I was serving as Dean on the faculty of a Canadian university, one of my responsibilities was to introduce prospective employers to those about to graduate. I recall the visit one day of the representative of a large chemical manufacturing company who was looking for suitable recruits. When I asked him whether he was simply interested in those taking a degree in the department of chemistry, his reply was: 'Not at all. Your chemistry students won't have learnt anything that will be of any use to them in our company. Whoever we employ will have to learn everything from scratch on the job. We are looking for people with initiative and imagination and we don't mind what department they come from. Put me in touch with some of your brightest people.'

Training for most jobs is best undertaken at the work place, not at school, polytechnic or university. This is the tradition of apprenticeship which today urgently needs reviving and expanding. One of the ways in which it is beginning to happen is in schemes such as the Youth Opportunities Programme and the Youth Training Scheme where unemployed young people are given work experience with suitable training, and a case can be made out for more flexibility in the school leaving age, allowing those whose bent is towards manual skills to concentrate on such activity rather than being compelled to sit in classrooms uninterested in the subjects they are supposed to learn. This approach is beginning to be adopted within many schools, but its success depends upon three things: first, a determination to base the curriculum on the needs of individual children, taking the stimulation of their interest and curiosity as the criterion of what is expected from them; second, a refusal to regard those with potential manual skills as failures and second-class citizens; third, the encouragement at later stages in life for people of all ages to take up subjects for which they were not ready in their early 'teens'. In passing, it is worth asking for how many the treasures of English literature and many other subjects have remained a closed book all their lives because their first introduction to them was a requirement which was regarded as a chore.

Of course, it would be absurd to argue that education has nothing to do with training for employment. However, its specific content has much less to do with what is needed for this purpose than we are commonly led to suppose. Those who intend to embark on a scientific or engineering career obviously require a background of factual knowledge which begins to be provided at school and is the basis for later courses at universities. But reliance on good examination results and academic degrees as necessary qualifications for offering a wide range of employment has by now distorted the whole educational process. Before the Second World War most of those embarking on a business career or entering professions such as the law or accounting never thought of going to a university in order to qualify for their future work. On leaving school they expected to learn on the job as trainees or articled clerks. Where professional examinations were required, they were taken alongside acquiring practical experience. Nowadays a university degree has come to be regarded as the *sine qua non* for securing any responsible position.

This is an unfortunate legacy we have taken over from North America where, long before the expansion of British universities, a college course was regarded almost as one of the human rights, not because of its inherent value, but because it was the social equivalent of 'keeping up with the Jones' and securing any decent job. As a consequence the universities were flooded with students who were not interested in the subjects they were supposed to study, content to secure the minimum pass degrees and enjoy the ride as far as they could. The absurd lengths to which this has gone is illustrated by a conversation I had with a door-to-door salesman who said he was going to register as an external student for a Canadian BA degree, not because he wanted to study any particular subject, but because without it he could not secure promotion in his employment.

A university should be a place of learning at an advanced level for those who are serious about it for its own sake. Entrance should be available to anyone who meets this qualification, but, if that were the criterion, the number of successful applicants would be drastically reduced. That is unlikely to happen as long as employers treat an academic degree as the test of a person's suitability for any kind of job. In the meantime the standards of excellence for which universities claim to strive are impaired by professors and lecturers spending time and energy on those who should not be there.

Such a judgment is of itself sufficiently controversial and likely to provoke an adverse reaction on the part of those who instinctively feel that different forms of provision for different people is to disadvantage some at the expense of others. That is what lies behind the introduction of the comprehensive system: the conviction that equality of opportunity requires the elimination of selection and mixed-ability classes. In many cases, however, streaming has proved inevitable and the division between grammar and secondary modern schools has been reproduced within the same comprehensive, while the constraints of examinations have led to the segregation of children into those capable of meeting the tests and those who are not. The fact is that the underlying principles have not been thought through, and equality of opportunity has been confused with similarity of provision. As long as education is graded hierarchically, with training in manual skills regarded as inferior to success in passing ordinary and advanced level examinations, and these standards inferior to university degrees, the champions of equality will aim at pushing as many as possible up the ladder whether they are ready for it or not. Hence the proliferation of institutions of higher education and the flooding of universities. Those who do not make the grade are thus condemned as failures. A Christian understanding begins from a different premise: the aim at ensuring the development of the full potentiality of every child; and that means recognizing the equal value of a variety of achievements. To put it in graphic form, the carpenter or the stone mason has as valuable a contribution to make to society as the PhD in English Literature. We should not be aiming at giving the same education to everybody, but the best education possible which is appropriate to the individual and his or her potentialities.

This leads to the whole question of examinations, the results of which are the password to most jobs for school leavers as well as to entrance for higher education. Their inadequacy for testing a pupil's ability is increasingly being recognized. They show what he or she is able to memorize, how far they have mastered the technique of answering a question paper in a restricted period of time, what foresight teachers have had of the questions likely to be asked and the luck of examinees in lighting on those for which they have been specifically prepared. They sometimes allow for showing critical judgment, though pupils are usually afraid of saying anything that they fear examiners will not expect. The result is very artificial and often misleading. Most candidates are under nervous strain and write under pressure; they may very well not do justice to themselves or make mistakes which in other circumstances they would not have done. Prospective employers need to ask whether the ability to achieve a high or a low mark under these conditions provides them with reliable information about the suitability of an applicant for the job on offer. It may give some information, but, generally speaking, an interview is far more revealing, especially when it is supported by honest references about general character and attainment. This is perhaps more widely appreciated than parents and even teachers commonly suppose.

The position is different as far as admission to further education is concerned. Here the attainment of good grades at the higher level is in general the necessary prerequisite for securing a place. Hence the school curriculum is in the last resort directed to that end. Nevertheless it is beginning to be realized that this method of selection, though apparently the fairest, does not necessarily indicate the real aptitude of the candidate for a course in higher education, and some universities are starting to place more emphasis on interviews and the reports of school heads. The problem with examinations is that, although they give some indication of *what* a candidate has learnt, they do not reveal *how* he or she has learnt it; and it is *how* someone learns that is crucial for their development: whether curiosity has been awakened, whether motivation has been enhanced, whether initiative has been evoked, and whether there is evidence of persistent self-discipline in the search for knowledge.

The examination system not only fails to provide this evidence, it actually militates against the young developing in this way. Faced with the demands to absorb pre-packaged material and to acquire the skill of making use of it in answering questions which can only be guessed in advance, there is little time or opportunity for them to follow their own interests or for teachers to encourage them to do so. Many learn what they will gratefully forget as soon as the examinations are over, having been prevented by the system from discovering the real rewards of exploring the subjects which they come to feel have been thrust down their throats. This does not mean that written tests should have no place whatsoever within the school curriculum; their real value lies in the assessment of a pupil's progress. But there is all the world of difference between an examination conducted internally to encourage achievement and a public ordeal which sets an arbitrary standard to make or break a child's prospects of advancement.

The argument of the foregoing paragraphs is likely to provoke a hostile reaction. Some will say that the case has been over-stated and that public examinations, whatever their imperfections, at least maintain standards of achievement and are the fairest way of determining the future direction of the school-leaver's career. Moreover, it will be argued that continuous assessment with reports on an individual's progress and dependence on interviews are highly subjective and may easily depend on the prejudices or faulty judgment of the teachers concerned and those engaged in the interviews of applicants for jobs or for places in institutions of further education. That cannot be denied. No system is perfect or free of problems. But we have to decide wherein the main advantages lie. In doing so, we have to recognize that, once a system has become established, it is very difficult to change. Many have a vested interest in its maintenance. The examination industry is now a powerful institution which for very human reasons would resist any inroads into its empire. More seriously, any change in the direction I have advocated would impose greater responsibilities on teachers which many would be loth to accept, and it would make considerable demands on their professional skill. It is much easier to have a set curriculum with examination targets than an open-ended programme adapted to the differing needs of individual children. Heads would argue that it would set them an impossible task given the quality and size of the teaching staff available to them.

For all these reasons I do not see the likelihood of any dramatic change in the immediate future, even if my general argument is regarded as persuasive. The most I could realistically hope for is a shift in emphasis and the steady erosion of the present system under pressure from the universities, which up to now have been largely responsible for the rigidities of the school curriculum. Added to that is the possible subversion of the system from within by individual teachers who see that as their vocation. To this I will return at the end of the chapter. Here I come back to the original question. The above critique of the place of examinations in the school curriculum arose from asking how far the British educational system is adapted to preparing young people for their future employment. For this purpose alone I believe it to be seriously defective because of the failure to make the right distinction between education and training. The distinction should not be too sharply drawn because in certain respects they overlap. As we have seen, a good deal of training can be done only effectively on the job. But in so far as education is a preparation for life, of which employment is an important part, it is concerned with providing the young with the tools which will enable them to do the jobs for which they are best fitted.

In some cases that means the encouragement of manual skills. In others it means learning how to acquire knowledge for the purpose of certain careers, as for example in science and engineering. For many more it involves the development of initiative and the motivation for learning where the accumulation of information and the study of particular subjects do not greatly matter. What a prospective employer needs to know is what sort of a *person* is applying for the job. Is he or she conscientious, reliable, capable of responding to a challenge, likely to work well with others, adaptable, eager to learn and to master whatever the job requires? It is the way in which the school experience is handled which provides the tools that count. Competence in history, geography, literature as such is not relevant. What matters is the *way* in which those subjects have been studied and the results in terms of the development of personality. Of course, the acquisition of skills in writing and expression are important as well as the ability to handle some of the new technology; and in this connection the introduction of computers into the classroom has provided a challenge to many youngsters which has helped to develop their potentiality. But the emphasis needs to be on stimulating interest and developing curiosity. That is the key to preparation for most jobs.

Nevertheless, to regard the business of education as primarily concerned with preparation for paid employment is an unduly narrow conception and, in so far as it becomes the controlling influence in the minds of either the parents or their children, it distorts the whole enterprise. When the question is asked 'What use is this subject to me?', the presumption behind it is almost invariably the belief that the only reason for studying anything is its supposed utility in ultimately securing a job. Teachers, a great majority of whom recognize that their profession has a wider objective – the preparation of the young for life – often find themselves severely constrained by these public expectations of what they are supposed to deliver. And yet, looking back on their experience, those interviewed in the surveys complained that the education they had received had not prepared them at all adequately for the world they encountered on leaving school.

Asked what they meant by this, many would list a number of things they did not know how to do: apply for jobs, fill up forms, conduct themselves at interviews, find the right sources of advice, handle their money and generally relate to an adult and complicated world. Many schools are doing their best to meet this sort of need, and often the complaints are grounded in the difference between talking about these things in the classroom and actually experiencing the problems and frustrations of coping with the situation the young face once the doors of the school are closed behind them. This is a way of saying that learning does not stop when formal education ends. However, after making allowance for the difference, there is much room for improvement, if the surveys do actually reflect a genuine sense of something seriously lacking. How many heads, for example, could honestly say that those leaving their schools had a basic understanding of how the governance of their communities work? At any rate, political ignorance is widespread and the whole democratic process suffers accordingly.

But this is only the tip of the iceberg. As I said at the beginning of the chapter, society is undergoing massive social change. Large numbers of school leavers are not finding jobs and those who do will enjoy opportunities for leisure far greater than their predecessors in former times. With the spread of television, video tapes and packaged entertainments of all kinds, there is a danger of producing a passive generation whose natural gifts will atrophy unless they are motivated to creative activity. This brings us back with fresh urgency to the central theme of this chapter. The crucial test of sound education is whether it stimulates curiosity and initiative, whether boys and girls are helped to see the possibilities of learning: the endless vista of a fascinating world to be explored. In so far as they are simply presented with a predetermined package of information which they are passively required to accept, they will be ill-prepared for creative living. Education is for life, for the development of potentiality which is never exhausted.

This suggests that for the future we have to look to a massive shift of resources to the expansion of adult education. Despite what I said earlier about the danger of the wrong people taking university courses for the wrong reasons, the potentiality of mature students for doing so should not be under-rated. In North America large numbers take degrees by extension, studying a variety of subjects over a number of years and building up the necessary total of credits. In the Canadian university where I taught, four times as many students were working for degrees in the evenings and summer schools than those registered for full-time courses. On the whole they proved to be much better prepared than school-leavers for embarking on subjects like philosophy, history, sociology and literature. In this country much has been done through such agencies as the Workers Educational Association and the extra-mural departments of the universities, which have themselves also begun to accept mature students, and the Open University has been an outstanding success. But this is only the beginning. Education is still widely regarded as the prerogative of the young. But in the changing society of the future continuing education, not just for qualifications or degrees, should be built into the expectations of everyone, starting with the seeds sown in schooldays.

So far I have said little except by implication about the main controversies regarding educational policy which have been in the forefront of the public debate: the role of government, the critique of selection, the responsibility of parents and independent as against state provision. Important as these questions are, they are secondary to what I have been discussing. Unless we are clear about the purpose of education as such, we shall be arguing from confused premises. But some answer must be given to these questions, bearing in mind what has already been said.

It is broadly agreed that government has a general responsibility for education. Controversy arises about how this should be exercised. The first thing to be emphasized is that educational policy is profoundly misconceived when it is used as a means of social control. This has to a considerable extent vitiated the whole debate about comprehensive schools. It is one thing to maintain that a certain type of school is in the best interests of children and offers the fullest opportunities for the development of their potentiality; it is another thing to attempt to use the educational system to change the structures of society. This has been the avowed purpose of some of the most eloquent political advocates of the abolishment of different types of school whether within the state sector or between the state sector and independent provision. It is held that what we have known in the past and what still obtains perpetuates class distinction and enhances the privilege of the few at the expense of the many. Only by making the same facilities available to all can social justice be done.

I do not want to repeat what I have already said earlier about the fallacy of trying to apply a mathematical notion of equality to what differentiates people from one another. Here I simply raise two questions. Is the class structure of British society actually changed by a rationalization of the school system and is education the proper tool for doing it anyway? People do group together in different social contexts; they live together in different neighbourhoods. One of the effects of the introduction of comprehensive schools has been to congregate children together from the same catchment area. That may have advantages in fostering a sense of community; it does nothing to break down the barriers between one catchment area and another. Only a mixture of population will do this, and that depends on housing, employment and a whole range of factors. The old grammar schools at least drew their pupils from a wide variety of social backgrounds. More importantly, we should ask whether the attempt to secure a social mix, if that can be done, is the main criterion for the kind of school we want for our children. It may be one of the things we would like to see, but, if I am right, the crucial question is what kind of school offers the best opportunity for the educational development of the child. He or she should not be the tool of social engineering.

The foregoing is not meant to beg the question of comprehensive or independent schools one way or the other. My plea, rather, is that educational considerations should be paramount and not submerged in the party political debate about how society should be ordered. I concede that a case can be made for arguing that the two are inextricably bound up together, but I believe that, while politicians battle out the merits of a classless as against a mixed society, educational considerations easily go by default. This contention was forcefully underlined by Sir Robert Birley, one of the wisest and most experienced educationalists of modern times, in an address delivered at Chatham House after his return from administering the reconstruction of education in the British zone of Germany after the end of the Second World War. 'I do not want it to be thought that I believe that the reform of a school system necessarily changes the nature of the schools, what is taught in them, and how it is taught. In fact, I regard the very prevalent modern view, that such reforms, especially when they are essentially social and not educational in their intent, will of themselves alter or improve the nature of a country's education, as a formidable modern heresy.'[2]

In the second place, questions arise about the relative responsibilities of national and local government in educational provision: a growing source of tension as central control of expenditure increasingly determines matters of policy. From the point of view of Whitehall it appears that one model for the provision of public services predominates, and that, though not generally admitted, is the organization of the defence of the realm. This is inevitably hierarchical, with planning in the hands of the service chiefs and diminishing responsibility devolved down the command structure to the private soldier, naval rating and airman who are required to do what they are told. Nobody would claim that it is the intentional model for relations between national and local government, but it may still have a dominant influence when the same chain of responsibility is assumed to be appropriate to public utilities and the provision of health, housing, social services and education.

Undoubtedly, it is a tidy model and one that appeals to the bureaucratic mind, but it is singularly inappropriate to education for which a strong case can be made in favour of turning the model upside down. Whatever the defects of the independent sector, one of its greatest strengths is the way in which schools are administered. Boards of governors with direct interest in the school concerned have the ultimate responsibility, and the actual administration is undertaken by a minimal staff under the direction of the headmaster or headmistress. In terms of economy this is obviously cost-effective, but it has the added advantage of localized involvement in the direction of the school's affairs. There is much to be said for seeing how far this can be carried in the public sector with as much responsibility as possible devolved to boards of governors on which parents, teachers and members of the local community most intimately connected with the school may serve. If block grants were allocated to such boards, they would be free to raise funds for special provisions: a practice that has recently come to be adopted in some places through the impact of centralized financial cuts. While the cuts may be deplored and their random incidence be manifestly harmful, local initiative can be a healthy compensatory factor which could be built into the system instead of being a response to an emergency. Of course, there would be all kinds of problems to be faced in reversing the chain of responsibility, not least because of the different resources available in different communities, and many mistakes would be made. But the merits of devolved responsibility and its practical consequences deserve to be seriously examined.

In the third place, Westminster has the ultimate responsibility of deciding the proportion of the national resources to be devoted to education at all levels. There are ominous signs that this is being done without due regard to social priorities. Quite apart from criticism that cash limits are fixed and cuts imposed without regard to educational criteria, it is doubtful whether a long-term strategy for the education of the nation is really on the planning horizon. If the balance between employment and leisure is undergoing a drastic change, those who look to the future need to see that we shall have to embark on a major expansion of educational provision, particularly, as I have already argued, for the adult population. Unless people are encouraged to learn throughout their lives, leisure will become boredom with dire social consequences, and retirement and old age a growing burden. It is economic sense, quite apart from anything else, to channel resources into stimulating creative activity rather than having to spend the nation's wealth on salvage and custodial care.

Nowhere has this been better stated than in a note at the end of Dorothy L. Sayers' statements of aims for a proposed series of Bridgehead books to initiate fresh thinking about society after the war. She maintained that the aims and methods of British education called for an entire overhaul. 'This is at present directed chiefly or wholly to the end of securing gainful employment, and is neither satisfactory in itself (i.e. in producing wise and happy citizens) nor even successful in its avowed purpose (i.e. it is powerless to check unemployment and does not fit people for the useful employment of leisure). The nation must be encouraged to take a very much wider view of the function of education, in better accordance with the needs of human nature and good citizenship, and to demand of its government that the necessary money for this better education shall be forthcoming. That is to say, that education which fits the citizen for peace must be taken at least as seriously as the armaments which fit him for war, and the necessary expenditure of thought and money cheerfully incurred.'[3] Forty years later these words are as pertinent as when they were first written.

To return to the schools. One unresolved problem is whether private education should be encouraged alongside the state system or whether social justice demands that this should be made difficult or even outlawed. Whatever view we take, we have to recognize the fact that more and more parents are sending their children to independent schools, paying extraordinarily high fees for doing so and therefore making considerable financial sacrifices into the bargain. There would be considerable resistance to any legislation which made this impossible. It would be argued that parents, not the state, have the ultimate responsibility for the welfare of their children, and that the government of the day has a case for interfering in their freedom of action only when it is publicly recognized that what they are doing is harmful to their children or seriously anti-social. It is doubtful whether a sufficiently strong case can be made out for that to justify prohibitive legislation.

This does not of itself imply that independent schools are desirable or to be encouraged. Parents send children to them believing that they are better than those in the state system. Whether they are is another matter. Some are and some are not. In so far as they provide an alternative method of education, offering special facilities, with a distinctive ethos and tradition, commanding the loyalty of old boys and girls and administered by a committed board of governors, the argument for their retention is a strong one. We cannot afford to lose any school which has something of value to offer on the ground that what everybody cannot enjoy should not be accessible to anyone at all. That is a prescription for grey mediocrity, and, if elevated into a general principle, would entail the loss of so much that enhances the quality of life for the nation as a whole. At the same time, the fact that entrance to independent schools depends on the ability of parents to pay does create a moral dilemma for those who maintain that education is so crucial to a child's development that the best, whatever it is, should be available to those most fitted for it irrespective of financial considerations. It is not like the possession of a work of art or living in a certain kind of house. It is a basic human right similar to equality before the law.

The arguments pull in opposite directions and I find it difficult to make more than a tentative judgment. Perfect justice is beyond human attainment in the kind of world in which we are living, and it is probably true that if we are to have schools of distinctive quality they will be provided only by those who are prepared to pay for them. In the last resort the independent sector has to justify itself by the excellence of what it provides. And here I have my doubts in so far as the so-called public schools which set the standard for private education reflect the managerial principles which infect the system as a whole. The test is how critical they are prepared to be of education which slots boys and girls into preconceived moulds rather than encourages their individual development. Almost every headmaster and headmistress would claim that this is what they aim to do, but the expectations of parents and society at large make this much more difficult than is commonly admitted.

This brings me to the heart of the matter. In the final analysis it is the quality of the teacher that counts. Never mind how splendid the buildings and excellent the equipment, how efficient the organization, how competitive the examination results, the real test of a school is whether members of the staff are themselves learners, exploring the field of knowledge beyond their present attainments, capable of sharing enthusiasm with the boys and girls entrusted to them, ready to stimulate and encourage every sign of curiosity which they can awaken. Still more important is their relationship to and expectations of their pupils. How far do they treat boys and girls as real people, not to be managed and manipulated, but as those whose trust and confidence has to be won? Here I revert to the third basic criticism uncovered by the two surveys. The overwhelming majority of those interviewed do not appear to have encountered teachers with this approach. They felt they were rarely treated as persons capable of responsible behaviour; they were regarded as kids who had to be kept in their place, dragooned into conformity by those who were afraid of losing their authority. Of course, that is not the whole story. Of course, there are many teachers scattered throughout the whole educational system whose attitude is markedly different. But I suspect that conversations in the average staff room would to a disturbing extent justify the reactions of the school leavers in the survey.

Before anyone jumps to the defence of the teaching profession and dismisses what I have said as a caricature, let it be acknowledged that the alternative approach to teacher-pupil relationships is immensely difficult to put into practice. Not only does it run counter to public expectations and the way in which these are built into the system; it calls for a degree of self-criticism and sensitivity against which frail human nature rebels. Anyone who recognizes the validity of an open approach to the young is bound to encounter the criticism of colleagues who have settled for an authoritarian role because that is the easier option, ministers to their self-esteem and does not make too great demands on their imagination. Everyone in every walk of life is tempted to settle into a rut and the teaching profession is no exception. It would be strange if a common reaction were not 'I've had twenty years experience and I know what children are like.' Even those who see their role in an entirely different way have a constant battle on their hands within themselves to keep open to growth and to have the patience and trust to win the confidence of the young and encourage their full potentiality.

Yet it can be done, and there are many in the public and the private sector who are doing it. That is where real education is taking place. Here is an obvious vocation for Christians who should have the inestimable advantage of knowing that self-criticism is built into the faith they profess as well as a commitment to the belief that every child has boundless potentiality in the sight of God. They may not live up to their vocation, but at least they have no excuse for not knowing what it is.

The discussion of education for living has provided an illustration of the relationship between the two levels of political action to which reference was made in the Preface. The state is responsible for maintaining the framework of education and for establishing the policies which govern it. This falls within the sphere of politics as commonly understood. I have argued that radical changes and new departures are required if education is really to be for living in a changing society. But whatever developments take place in the system as a whole, they will not necessarily touch the heart of the matter which is the approach of the teacher to his or her professional responsibility. Ultimately education is not dictated in Whitehall or County Hall or even on a board of governors. Nor is it entirely in the hands of school heads, important as their influence may be. In the last resort it takes place in the classroom, in the relationship between a teacher and a group of boys and girls. That is where effective political action is taken in the broader sense of public responsibility for what happens. We have been too easily mesmerized into thinking that results are only achieved by campaigning to change the system. Without denigrating the importance of this in the field of education as much as in any other social concern, the individual teacher can achieve much whatever the system; and in education what the teacher achieves is really what matters. As one of the most experienced and imaginative of them said in the course of a conversation leading up to the writing of this chapter, 'As a Christian I am profoundly critical of the assumptions which underlie the system within which I operate. But rather than spend my time and energy campaigning for changes in it, I can do much more by undermining the system from within by the way in which I approach boys and girls and the expectations I have of them.' That may well be the most effective political action: a strategy of which many radicals might not approve. But an ounce of achievement is worth a ton of frustrated talking.

7

A Caring Community

The twentieth century has seen a dramatic expansion in the role of government for the provision of social welfare. Until recently this has been generally taken for granted as a natural evolution to a more civilized society, but, with the return of a Conservative administration in 1979, the debate began to be joined between those who believed that the process had gone too far or at least had reached its limits and those determined to defend what had been achieved and build upon it for the future. The crux of the argument has turned on the management of public expenditure. Should this be cut, and, if so, by how much and by what means? Or should it be expanded? In the resultant controversy, the purpose for which finance should be made available and the values determining policy have not been exposed to sufficiently rigorous scrutiny. It is easier to deal in figures than ask uncomfortable questions, especially if these begin to disturb entrenched shibboleths.

Nobody can dispute that huge strides have been made in tackling poverty and disease since the nineteenth century. The novels of Charles Dickens, for example, depict scenes of misery in the great cities which now seem like the dark ages. Whatever our contemporary problems, the extreme manifestations of squalor which the Victorians were so slow to recognize and tackle are a matter of the now almost unbelievable past. It is even difficult for most people today to appreciate that in the lifetime of our older citizens the sight of children in rags with no shoes or stockings was a commonplace. Hunger and disease stalked the mean streets of our major cities right up to the outbreak of the Second World War.

Throughout the Victorian era the relief or distress was a local responsibility, mainly left in the hands of voluntary charitable organizations, the pioneering character of which began to arouse the sleeping conscience of the nation. The most that these organizations could achieve was ambulance work, and the demands of social reformers, like Frederick Denison Maurice and John Stuart Mill, to get to the roots of the problem largely fell on deaf ears. Mill had pleaded for measures to overcome poverty, disease and all deprivation.[1] But the country was not yet ready for that. However, in the teeth of complacency and indifference, the legislators at Westminster were compelled to face the necessity for government action at least in limited fields. For example, obligatory primary education was introduced and the factory acts controlling the exploitation of children were placed on the statute book. Nevertheless this was a far cry from the recognition that the nation as a whole had a responsibility for the welfare of all its citizens and still further from an acceptance of the right of every man, woman and child to the true dignity of a human being. The image of the Lady Bountiful held almost unchallenged sway; the prosperous had a responsibility to help the deserving poor, the implication being that much of the grinding poverty was the fault of those who were too feckless to do anything for themselves. Even those described as deserving charity were regarded as inferior to those who gave it, expected to be grateful for the munificence of those who generously donated a fraction of their wealth to relieve the distress of others. Class consciousness dominated the interpretation of the voluntary principle and most of those motivated by it were not ready to face the need for radical structural changes if poverty and the deprivation which went with it were to be effectively tackled.

Of course, there were exceptions. The story is told of a minister's wife in the East End of London before the First World War who was told of a family with a new-born baby where there was no food at all in the house. She tucked a golden sovereign inside her glove and set out to find the address. Instead of taking the direct route, she made a circuitous way through the dismal streets trying to put off the moment when she feared that she would have to put another human being in a humiliating position. At last she found the house and heard a baby crying from hunger. Somehow she brought herself to knock at the door, and, when it was opened, managed to get the sovereign from out of her glove and into the hands of a despairing woman. With cheeks aflame with shame that anyone should be so beholden to another, she made her way home and cried herself to sleep. That sovereign was repaid many times over on the anniversary of the gift to help somebody else in similar need.

I have told the story as I heard it from the person concerned. It illustrates a sensitive Christian response to what was seen as an intolerable situation. But it was an approach hard for anyone to sustain, even for herself, in a climate in which philanthropy was commonly practised in terms of condescension. It has to be confessed that for the most part Christians reflected the prevailing attitudes of the time. To see injustice in its effect on real people, as distinct from a theoretical problem, requires as much effort of the imagination today as it did at the turn of the century.

The tide had to turn. Government action had become imperative. Moreover, the rise of the Trade Union and Labour movements meant that those who represented the underprivileged began to demand that the poor had a right to a decent standard of living. They were not to be regarded as the recipients of state or private charity, but as those who were claiming their rightful place in the body politic. For many this involved such a radical change in attitude that it was slow to become established. Even today Victorian standards still prevail though generally camouflaged in plausible political slogans.

The first effective steps pointing the way forward were taken by Lloyd George's pre-First World War Liberal government with the introduction of unemployment benefit and old age pensions. But that only began to break up the ground. The first comprehensive effort to tackle the problem of social deprivation arose out of a fresh sense of national solidarity occasioned by the shared trials of the Second World War. These laid the foundations on which the concept of the Welfare State was based, spelt out in the Beveridge report at the instigation of Churchill's coalition government, the provisions of which were enacted by the Labour administration under Clement Attlee from 1945 onwards.

On leaving the University, the young Beveridge was told by Edward Caird, the Master of Balliol, 'When you have learned all that Oxford can teach you . . . go and discover why, with so much wealth in Britain, there continues to be so much poverty, and how poverty can be cured.'[2] That was the task Beveridge set himself, and the result was the famous report with which his name will always be associated. He identified five giants which were to be confronted and overthrown: want, disease, squalor, ignorance and unemployment. By the end of the war something had been done about education with the passing of the Butler Act of 1944. But it was the new administration which had to implement the sweeping proposals which Beveridge made by the introduction of a comprehensive scheme of social security and the establishment of the National Health Service in which Aneurin Bevan played such a leading role. Nevertheless, it was the much under-estimated Attlee who steered through a programme of legislation which decisively changed the framework of British politics and which entitles his administration to the verdict of the greatest reforming government of the century. It is said that Attlee was described by Churchill as 'a sheep in sheep's clothing'. The judgment of history will be in the sharpest contradiction to that.

Beveridge, however, saw his proposals as providing only the framework, or perhaps more accurately the foundation for a more just society. In retrospect he came to be profoundly unhappy with the image conjured up in the minds of most people by the report of which he had been the author, and in particular with the notion of the Welfare State as the universal provider of all that people required.[3] He believed that he had done no more than propose a safety net which would ensure that nobody suffered from extreme deprivation: a safety net which would release the energies of the whole population to build a more caring and mutually responsible society. This is how he described his blueprint: 'A minimum only, it leaves room and incentive to individuals to add to it for themselves according to their personal capacities and desires.'[4] Later in the concluding passage of his book on *Voluntary Action* he wrote: 'We must continue to use to the full the spirit that made our great organizations for mutual aid and that fired the philanthropists of the past.'[5] The need for private enterprise – not in business – but in the service of mankind, he believed, was beyond debate. At the end of his life Beveridge had come to fear that his vision had been lost in the assumption that the state could be the universal provider.

Had he been alive today, Beveridge might well have felt that his worst fears had been realized, though he might also have seen the crisis of confidence in the workings of the Welfare State as an opportunity for rethinking the enterprise to which he devoted so much of his life. Poverty remains a blight on the national landscape; unemployment has risen once more to pre-war proportions; squalor spreads at the heart of many of our cities; education at all levels is subject to severe cuts and the whole system is due for overhaul, as I maintained in the previous chapter; the National Health Service is thought by many to be crumbling; and the social services are being strained to the utmost to provide the community care which the population has come to expect. Nevertheless, the framework erected by the post-war Labour government remains. If it is creaking or even beginning to break apart, there is no thought of going back to pre-Beveridge days. The Welfare State may not have fulfilled the expectations of its pioneers; there may be much that is wrong with it in the way in which it has developed. But that is no reason for abandoning the concept or for minimizing the substantial achievements of Attlee, Bevan and their colleagues. The imperative now is to learn from past mistakes and to chart a constructive way foward to a society in which mutual responsibility is given expression in structures which raise the quality of life for everyone.

What went wrong? After the General Election of 1970 a Labour back-bencher who had just retired was asked whether he would miss being out of the House of Commons. 'Oh no,' he replied. 'I'm glad to be out of it. We've created expectations which we could not possibly fulfil.' That lies somewhere near the heart of the problem. There are limits to what any government can do, and when the expectation has been created that it can do anything, that only lack of sufficient resolve or incompetence prevents the achievement of any desired goal, disillusionment is bound to set in, and public disenchantment with the whole democratic process results. The most frequent criticism of politicians is that they make promises in order to get elected which they fail to redeem when in office. This is partly the fault of the politicians themselves and partly of the electorate, which has come to expect far more of them than they can possibly deliver.

This has been notably the case in respect to the ideal of the Welfare State. Too little thought has been given to the precise limitations of central government. The debate has been conducted on the generalized plane of more or less government action, while underlying questions of what exactly is its proper function have largely gone by default. To pose those questions is not necessarily to swing the generalized debate one way or the other. It means asking what a government department can effectively do and how it can best be done.

The most obvious limitation on the effectiveness of central government provision in the field of public welfare is the inevitable bureaucracy with its plethora of regulations which is required to administer any national programme. Bureaucracy has become a dirty word largely because the individual citizen so often finds himself frustrated by the network of regulations, form-filling and officials through which he has to penetrate to secure adequate consideration of his own special needs. Many give up and settle for resentful criticism of the whole system. But if anything is to be done on a very large scale, bureaucracy is inevitable. It is not the fault of malicious or insensitive politicians and civil servants; it is the only way in which government can operate. Of course, bureaucracy can be streamlined and made more flexible; its procedures can and should be kept under constant and critical review; most important of all, those engaged in it should be continually reminded of the purposes they exist to promote. Too often, as I have already said, administrative convenience becomes the controlling factor rather than the fulfilment of stated objectives and meeting the diversity of human needs. That is perhaps the most valid general criticism of the civil service, and one which has to be continually pressed home. But when all this has been taken into account, bureaucratic procedures are unavoidable when anything has to be organized on a large scale. There are certain responsibilities which obviously fall into this category: the defence of the realm is one of them, and in the social sphere all provisions which have to be uniformally applied across the whole nation, such as standards of health and safety at places of work, the administration of the law, and so on. But the Welfare State was initiated and developed at a time when it was taken for granted that 'Large is Beautiful', or, if not beautiful, obviously efficient. As a consequence, the whole field of public welfare was planned from the top downwards, the unconscious model being the armed services, as I argued in the last chapter when dealing with education.

The assumptions lying behind this development are now ripe for being called in question. For one thing, those who make mistakes in planning large scale enterprises can multiply the results to staggering proportions. I recall the Dean of Engineering joining me for coffee one morning in the university refectory with a broad smile on his face. 'I've left them to it,' he said, 'the architect, the contractor, the sub-contractor and the clerk of works. They've made the same mistake in the piping of the new engineering building 650 times over.' That was a mistake multiplied in one large building; but what disastrous results follow from a major error in planning construction spread over a whole city, let alone a whole country? That is what happened in the design of high-rise apartment blocks to deal with the rehousing of the British population after the damage done during the war. The planners failed to take into account how people actually live together if they are to constitute any sort of community. The comradeship of the street with its back-to-back houses, doorsteps for gossiping and little corner shops was replaced by towers of concrete: admittedly better built for the most part (Roman Point was an exception) and with far better physical amenities, but wholly unsuitable for bringing up families, overcoming loneliness and isolation, and recreating community. The complaint of an old lady that the council had buried her seven stories above the ground speaks for itself. Now tower blocks, built at enormous public expense only a few years ago, are having to be demolished because people will not live in them. Victims of vandalism and even muggings in stair wells and elevators, many have rebelled against the anonymity of the apartments they were compelled to occupy. The planners had simply not taken real people into account.

This is a particularly striking example of how large-scale planning can go wrong and its mistakes be multiplied through not being in close enough touch with people where they actually are in all their variety. If the expanding size of an organization, with its inevitable bureaucracy, is no longer the necessary touchstone of efficiency and productiveness in industry, by how much more must this be the case with the provision of social welfare which has to do with the needs of an individual, a family or a small community? If we start with them, the perspective is very different, and the judgment on central government may be not that it fails to deliver what is required, but that it is inherently incapable of doing so because of its remoteness from the daily concerns of ordinary people. This is not a criticism or a complaint; it is simply a statement of fact. To avoid misunderstanding, I am not suggesting that central government has no role to play in the field of social welfare – far from it – but that its scope is strictly limited to what can be effectively organized on a large scale. What that is then becomes a matter for debate.

Here the argument about the relative responsibilities of central and local government begins to take off. Is the answer to the problem of the large-scale operations of central government the devolution of even more responsibility for social welfare to regional and district councils than the considerable amount they already have? Representing very varied situations, local councillors claim to stand nearer to the people than Westminster or Whitehall. They argue that it is for them to decide what needs to be done and to have the ability to require the revenue from rates and central government support grants to do it. At the time of writing, this claim has been reinforced in the controversy about measures being taken to control local government expenditure. Councillors of every political persuasion up and down the country are fiercely arguing that if central government takes responsibility for fixing the spending limits of local authorities, this virtually takes away their power of deciding what is in the interests of the community they serve.

In the heat of the argument the case can be and is over-stated. Setting ceilings to revenue does not remove all discretion from local councillors, and it is an exaggeration to say that rate-capping is the end of local government. Within the limits prescribed, priorities still have to be settled at the council level. But monetary control is a clumsy weapon, and, when applied on a large-scale, diverts attention from the merits or otherwise of a particular policy. It is a rough and ready means for the apportionment of resources which cannot possibly allow for all the local variations and the perceived priorities of those who stand nearest to the scene. On the other hand, the immediate reaction of councillors to cuts in the rate support grant or rate-capping with the claim that more money, not less, should be at their disposal may also be a way of avoiding a clear, hard look at what needs to be done and the best method of doing it. Pouring extra money into the Health Service or education is not of itself a prescription for improvement; if it were forthcoming, it might make reforms more difficult to achieve. However, to start with money rather than with people and their welfare is to begin in the wrong place, and this is the substance of the case currently being made by the Association of Local Authorities against the strict financial controls being imposed by the government in Whitehall.

Nevertheless, this does not settle the argument in favour of local government. In the light of experience, we are entitled to ask whether too much is expected of it and too large claims made on its behalf. Councillors and their officials are naturally resistant to any curtailment of their powers, but their argument that they are in a unique position to respond to local needs conceals an element of self-delusion. Are they as closely in touch with the people they represent as they claim to be? Much evidence points the other way. Only a small proportion of those entitled to do so bother to vote in local elections, and those who do appear to be more influenced by the national party debate than by local issues. Few people know the name of their councillor or would recognize him if they met him in the street. They are much more likely to be able to put a name and face to their member of parliament to whom they have readier access through the surgeries conducted within the constituency, while the party caucus on the local council so often presents the image of a secret society impervious to penetration. Of course, there are exceptions, and I have dealt in broad generalities. But the way in which many people speak of 'the council' betrays an alienation from local government even greater than is felt from the proceedings at Westminster. The problem of involving people in the direction of their own affairs and in taking responsibility for the welfare of the community in which they live is as much a challenge to local as to national government. This does not mean that the case for devolution of responsibility from London to the regions and localities is in any way weakened, or that lower tiers of government are not in a better position to assess certain priorities and effectively administer programmes of public welfare. All that I am saying is that the bureaucracy of scale is also a limitation on the effectiveness of County or City Hall, compounded by the caucus-like operations of the political parties in local government. The question needs to be asked at all levels: what is it reasonable and desirable to expect of elected representatives? The answer may turn out to be 'a good deal more in some respects and a good deal less in others'. At all events the bureaucratic structure of the Welfare State calls for a critical reappraisal of what it can and should be expected to deliver.

Perhaps the most serious thing that has gone wrong with the evolution of the Welfare State is the growing attitude of dependency which it has generated. Many people have come to regard the state as a sort of guardian who should take care of them from birth to death, who is blessed with endless resources for doing so, and in fact behaves in a miserly way by being penny-pinching. The Lady Bountiful of the Victorian era is replaced by the image of an unnecessarily insensitive fairy godmother. The concept of a nation-wide co-operative venture to eliminate obstacles to the emergence of a responsible society has been replaced by a 'them and us' mentality which is a far cry from the ideas of Beveridge and the motivation of the early pioneers who fought for a recognition of the dignity of everyone whatever their circumstances might be.

Unhappily politicians have been in no small measure responsible for this outcome, especially where they have long been in undisputed control of a local council. Some time ago I was a member of a small group of churchmen who went to see the leaders of a city council to ask what contribution they thought the churches could and should make to the life of the community. The assumptions of both parties turned out to be so diametrically opposed that dialogue never really started. The Labour councillors assumed that we were simply interested in how the churches could be strengthened, pews filled and memberships increased. They insisted on confining themselves to suggestions about how the churches could become more popular! When asked about participation in the affairs of the city, in the improvement of the quality of life of those who lived there, they made it quite plain that this was their business in which they wished no interference, not simply on the part of the churches but on the part of the population as a whole. Their attitude was that they had been elected to provide the services which the city required and they did not expect anyone to take any responsibility beyond casting the votes which periodically returned them to office. Towards their constituents they betrayed a paternalism which made the Victorian Lady Bountiful look like a radical reformer by comparison. This may have been an extreme case occasioned by too long a period of unchallenged power and uncriticized assumptions, but it illustrates an attitude which has taken deep root in British society.

The time has come for fresh thinking about the Welfare State: thinking that goes beyond the common assumptions of the political right and left and the sterile confrontation resulting therefrom. Christians have a contribution to make to this, based upon the conviction that human destiny lies in fraternity, in co-operation rooted in mutual responsibility in which everybody has a part to play according to their several gifts. This seems to me to challenge the adequacy of much current analysis of the role of the state in the promotion of social welfare.

A fruitful place to start is a very frank interview between Margaret Thatcher and Brian Walden on television in January 1984. Asked to explain her policy on the control of public expenditure and the reduction of taxation, the Prime Minister emphasized that she was concerned to reduce the scope of state activity and allow more money for people to spend out of their own pockets as they wished. Pressed on what were the necessary responsibilities of central government, she gave priority to national defence and the preservation of law and order, while holding the present ceiling on expenditure for health and social welfare. The impression was left on the viewer that the Prime Minister regarded public expenditure as a necessary evil and that the plight of the poor, the homeless and the unemployed could be treated as a statistical problem kept in check by the forces of law and order. I hope this is not too harsh a judgment, but it is almost inevitable when freedom for people to spend their own money on themselves becomes the dominant theme. There was no indication in the interview of any constructive thinking about what the state should do to provide a more adequate framework for social advance and still less any apparent appreciation of the responsibility of the individual citizen for the welfare of his neighbours. People were to be set free from the restrictions of state provision not in order that they might find ways of co-operating with one another for the promotion of the common good, but in order that they might satisfy their desires for increasing consumption.

The reaction of the political left to this whole approach is to condemn it as lacking in compassion and sensitivity towards a large section of the population, while ministering to the instincts of selfishness and greed which are never far from the surface and ready to be exploited for political ends. The Left sees the state as having the positive role of raising the standards of life for everyone, with priority given to the poor, the sick and the underprivileged. But there too the analysis so often stops. Instead of asking what the state can most appropriately do and how the energies of people may be released and encouraged to take responsibility for social advancement, government is seen as the universal provider. Thus confrontation is at the unproductive level of whether there should be more or less state responsibility and more or less public expenditure, whereas the much more important questions are *what* should be the task of government, centrally, regionally and locally, and *how* responsibility should be devolved to as many people as possible for the welfare of their own communities.

Taking this as the point of departure, we may go back to Beveridge and ask in what way the vision he had of a national framework of welfare within which a thousand flowers could bloom can be realistically applied in the closing decades of this century. As I have already said, he saw the role of central government to be tackling the five giants of want, disease, squalor, ignorance and unemployment. That requires reasserting and governments are to be judged by the yardstick of whether they produce general policies which harness the resources of the nation to achieve these ends. As we look back on what has happened since the end of the war, the picture is a chequered one. More progress has been made in some areas than in others. In some instances the detailed application of policy has become a jungle of confusion, while in others, like unemployment, there has been virtual abandonment of the professed ideal.

To begin with the war on want, it is obviously impossible to give any precise definition of the standard to which a civilized society should be aiming. People's needs vary and wants in the sense of desires can be insatiable. When Beveridge talked about the elimination of want he was speaking of the kind of major deprivation which reduced living to a bare struggle for existence. The necessities of food, clothing, warmth and housing should be guaranteed to everybody. This is an area where patchy progress has been made. Hunger has been virtually eliminated; nobody needs to go around without adequate clothing; social security benefits ensure some income to everyone. But the framework of provision has become hopelessly complicated: so much so that large numbers of people do not know the benefits to which they are entitled or how to obtain them. The social security system has to be nationally organized and funded and it is within that framework that the social services can be developed through local initiative, but the system urgently requires simplification; and that is the business of central government.

This is largely an administrative problem. It is different with housing. Here the record contains a catalogue of failure in three respects: first in the lack of urgency with which successive governments have applied themselves to the problem; second, in the disastrous mistakes of planners and their lack of imagination, to which reference has already been made; and third, in inadequately thought-out policies of new buildings, home-ownership and home-improvement. And the mistakes have not just been made in the past. The prospect for the future is even bleaker. An article in *The Times* in December 1983 warned that the number of houses unfit for human habitation or lacking basic amenities or in urgent need of repair is rapidly growing, and by 1991 could double to 2¼ million. The policy of encouraging home ownership by the sale of council houses is running into serious difficulties because with high mortgages the cost of repairs is beyond the means of many of those who have acquired aging property, and we face a situation in which waiting lists for housing will lengthen to the extent that some will have no hope of a home of their own in their lifetime.[6] Instead of tackling squalor, as Beveridge urged, we are in process of spreading it, because it is largely deterioration in housing that causes squalor, even if it is compounded by pollution of the environment and the spread of ugliness in industrial and public buildings. A home is a basic human need. Without it family life is impossible. If it is damp, deteriorating, dismal and badly designed in itself and in relation to its neighbourhood, it provides the background for every social problem. To neglect the proper housing of the people or to give it low priority in public expenditure is to store up incalculable costs for the future.

Central government's responsibility is to secure the funds necessary for a major attack on the housing problem. Local authorities are in the best position to identify what needs to be done and to administer the expenditure, but here the involvement of the occupier is crucial. They are the people who live in the dwellings and every small co-operative, such as a housing or tenants association, has a contribution to make in ensuring that people take responsiblity for where they live. Those who can meet the costs of purchase, mortgages and improvements should do so, but where it is evident that resources are insufficient the nation as a whole has an essential part to play. Failure to grasp this nettle by giving reduction in taxation priority over doing so is economic folly and a prescription for social disintegration. It is nothing less than a dereliction of duty on the part of central government.

Failure to meet the challenge of unemployment has been the most obvious retreat from Beveridge's concept of public welfare. Conditions have changed since the 1940s. What then appeared to be a relatively straightforward problem to tackle, given sufficient resolution, has become a much more complex matter through the changing pattern of world trade, the oil crisis and general economic recession. Successive governments have been caught unprepared for the major changes they had to face. The Thatcher administration has claimed that all it can do is to create the context within which economic growth can take off and new jobs be created. This is part of the truth, though the argument that a programme of expenditure on house building, public works and the infrastructure would be non-inflationary and mitigate the problem of unemployment is a compelling one. However, the real challenge to government is to rethink the whole concept of work and productive activity, and that has scarcely begun. The framework for which it is responsible is not just the financial and economic structure within which business and the manufacturing and service industries have to operate, but the initiation of fresh thinking about the balance between paid work and leisure in a different kind of society from that to which we have been traditionally accustomed.

The greatest success in the broad provision of public welfare has been the National Health Service. In some places it has functioned excellently, providing a full coverage of treatment for all types of illness without imposing additional financial burdens on those who have benefitted from it. General accessibility to a doctor and a hospital has been a tremendous, though costly, achievement. But there have been problems and they are becoming more acute. Waiting lists for some operations have lengthened to proportions where people have suffered pain and disability for months and sometimes years on end. In the big cities, doctors' lists have become overcrowded and patients have often felt that insufficient time has been given them to be treated as persons, rather than as cases to be rushed in and out of the consulting room. In the face of this, when financial cuts are made, wards are closed and staff reduced, the cry goes up for more money to be spent. There is more than a little justification for the view that this presupposes a bottomless state purse and that the availability of ever larger quantities of money would not necessarily improve the service. It is the very size of the system that now creates the problems, as anyone knows who has been a patient in hospital and has experienced the frustration of doctors and nurses with the top-heavy and cumbersome administration to which they are subject. Moreover, there is a widespread suspicion that, in spite of all the protestations that the welfare of the patient comes first, the system works in the interests of the administrators, the consultants and the hospital staff.

All generalized criticisms are bound to be unfair. The important thing is to identify what is going wrong and precisely where it is going wrong, and that becomes progressively harder to do when the administration assumes massive proportions and thereby becomes increasingly inflexible. The case for a breakdown of responsibility to the most localized units is a powerful one together with the involvement of voluntary agencies in the provision of ancillary facilities and the raising of special funds for particular purposes in their own hospital. One example of what might be done, as I have indicated earlier, is the expansion of state-funded beds in privately-run nursing homes for geriatric patients, releasing hospital wards to reduce the waiting lists for hip operations, hernias and the like. Rigid views about the way patients should be treated and the auspices under which this should be done may satisfy the professional associations and trade unions by safeguarding their own prerogatives, but it may do so at the actual expense of the sick. The National Health Service is a clear example of the requirement to begin planning from the standpoint of the individual patient and not from that of the administrator in Whitehall.

I have already said something about education where again the case for turning the large-scale administrative model upside down is particularly apposite. I do not need to repeat that here. However, it is when we come to the social services that the importance of the widest possible local participation is most obviously paramount. The sheer variety of personal needs and the opportunities for the improvement of the life of every community cannot possibly be covered by statutory arrangements. It has long been recognized that in this the voluntary organizations have an important function. They are not bound by strict regulations and they are able to supplement the provision of local authorities by filling in the gaps. With the imposition of financial ceilings, it has become apparent that the expansion of statutory social services has reached its peak. While the local authorities have to provide the infrastructure and maintain as far as they can the institutions and professional and paid services which have so far been established, the scope for voluntary effort is unbounded. Loneliness is one of the major social problems, and that can best be met by the friendly neighbour, the quality of whose own life is enhanced by the contribution the lonely person makes to her. The young can help the old to their mutual advantage. All kinds of services can be rendered, clubs and associations formed, tenants groups organized and new projects initiated. The Liberal Party's stress on community politics is designed not only to open up the Local Authority to wider participation by the people, but to encourage them to take responsibility for the neighbourhood to which they belong. The much lamented cuts in statutory social services could lead to a healthy burgeoning of such voluntary efforts. We need a new approach to social welfare. Instead of a grudging admission that certain things need to be done to relieve distress, we should see co-operative effort and mutual responsibility to improve the quality of life for everyone as the way to human fulfilment. In this, central government, local government and all the voluntary agencies have their part to play, not in tension with one another, but in organic relationship. Towards this fresh and positive attitude Christians have an important contribution to make, based upon their understanding of what human society is meant to be. But it could be a disturbing contribution to established practice if spelt out in what are likely to be seen as three highly controversial propositions, in which I draw together recurring themes throughout these chapters.

The first is that responsibility should be devolved as far as that is practicable. Central government should not try to control what can be handled by local authorities and the latter should look as far as possible to voluntary agencies for the promotion of social welfare. The first half of this proposition is likely to win wider acceptance than the second because there is considerable resistance to the centralization of powers. That inevitably means the generalization of provision whereas the needs of people in different localities vary. Those whose concern is with a particular borough, city or district should have the widest discretion in deciding what is in the best interests of those whom they represent. It is one thing for Westminster to require local authorities to take responsibility for education and the social services; it is another to tell them how to do it. The maximum unscrambling and unloading from the ministries in Whitehall to the County and Town Halls should be the order of the day.

More controversial is likely to be the suggestion that they in their turn should not attempt to do what can be tackled by voluntary agencies. For a long time it has worked the other way. The Welfare State has been taken to require as much statutory provision as resources would allow. In many cases voluntary agencies have been treated with suspicion, almost as if their very existence was an implied criticism of the local authority for not doing its job properly. To reverse that and positively encourage voluntary initiative would require a fundamental change of attitude on the part of many local politicians. But if they argue the case as they do for greater freedom from Whitehall and wider discretion in the exercise of their powers, they should face the claim that their own responsibilities should be restricted and devolved to as many people as possible.

The second proposition is that a way should be found of transferring the raising of revenue to those who have the responsibility for administering it. Without that, devolution of responsibility cannot be fully implemented. Everyone is agreed that our tax and rating systems are profoundly unsatisfactory and in urgent need of complete overhaul, but no government has yet succeeded in doing anything about it. Hence the impasse which has arisen over local government finance. If councillors are to be responsible for expenditure within their districts, they must be accountable to those who provide the revenue, and while the major part of this comes from rate support grants, arbitrarily allocated by Whitehall, and the rest from levies upon only a proportion of the electorate, there is no proper accountability to the electing and benefitting constituency. The result is a direct clash between responsibility for providing services and accountablility for public expenditure. The introduction of local taxation seems to be the only way of getting to grips with the problem, though it bristles with administrative difficulties. In so far as these stem from the reluctance of Treasury officials to allow for inroads on their empire, this must be resisted. In so far as the problems are administrative, they should be overcome. The outcry against reductions in the rate support grants and proposals for controlling the freedom of local authorities to fix their own level of rates will not subside until there has been a drastic change in policy. The case for regional and local taxation is now overwhelming.

The third and most controversial proposal is that there should be a concerted effort to change attitudes towards rates, taxes and public expenditure. We have long been conditioned to think that whenever possible they are to be avoided and that their reduction is an obviously desirable goal. But why should it be thought that money spent on co-operative ventures to improve the quality of community life should be discouraged while spending sprees at the January sales or large outlays on gambling and amusement arcades are somehow economically advantageous to the nation? When representatives of the Institute of Directors appear on television before Budget Day, urging the Chancellor of the Exchequer to reduce taxation in order that people may have more in their pockets to buy goods in the shops, their own interest as manufacturers is understandable. But when this is presented as being in the national interest as the way to raise the standard of living and secure more employment, viewers are being subjected to a confidence trick. Who, for example, can seriously maintain that repairing our dilapidated houses, improving our health, caring for the lonely, the old and the handicapped is a bad use of money compared with frittering it away on satisfying passing whims of fancy? I believe that Christians have to say that expenditure on corporate efforts to improve the quality of life take precedence over individual disposal of income for selfish purposes.

Acceptance of that means a willingness to support the raising of taxes nationally and locally where necessary, though the proposals for devolution of responsibility and the encouragement of voluntary community projects should actually mean an overall reduction in taxation. Whether that be so or not, Christians surely have a duty to be in the vanguard of a campaign to change public attitudes, to pay their own rates and taxes without grumbling or resentment and to advocate their increase where the public interest requires it. Of course, wastage has to be watched, exposed and ruthlessly criticized; sometimes the purposes to which public expenditure is devoted have to be called in question, especially whenever extravagant schemes are undertaken for the prestige or personal interest of those who initiate or operate them. But the general priority of corporate expenditure now needs asserting by all those who place the welfare of the community above private, selfish interests. That is undoubtedly to swim against the tide of natural inclination for Christians no less than for anybody else. As such it is the consequence of original sin, and has to be combatted, not fatalistically accepted. Nevertheless, every sign of altruism and generosity offers encouragement for believing that the tide is not irresistible. A fresh attitude to taxation might even create the climate for a growing sense of responsibility for voluntary contributions to social projects for which large sums of money are already raised. Rightly understood, taxation provides the infrastructure for voluntary effort.

I am under no illusion. None of the three proposals would be likely to make much headway without massive resistance. Even when proposals are widely accepted in theory, institutions and established procedures are extremely slow to respond. The larger the bureaucratic network, the more difficult it is to make any impression on it. Quite apart from the fact that each person in the network is likely to be defensive about his or her own job and the accustomed way of doing it, the inter-connection of individual pockets of resistance makes any substantial change very hard to achieve. The operation of the Soviet system is an obvious example. Many people seem to think that the men in the Kremlin exercise almost unrivalled power. The reverse is probably the truth. They are the prisoners of a huge bureaucracy which has spread like a web throughout the Soviet lands, rendering any individual, however highly placed, virtually powerless to alter anything. That is why the Soviet economy stagnates and its social life ossifies.

The only corrective to this is the gradual breakdown of the bureaucracies. To achieve it requires patience and determination. But first a growing number of people have to become convinced that this is what needs to be done. In the terms of the discussion of the foregoing pages, there is a strong case for the devolution of powers from Westminster and Whitehall to the regions and districts and with that the encouragement of every kind of voluntary enterprise. For as bureaucracy is broken down and units of co-operation become smaller, new possibilities of inter-personal initiative become released and a thousand flowers can begin to bloom.

8

The Wider Context

In arguing the case in the second chapter for devolution of powers, I briefly touched on the need for advocating this in more than one direction: upwards from national government to international agencies as well as downwards to regional and localized authorities. If the latter meets with resistance, that is nothing compared with the reluctance of governments all over the world to surrender anything that affects their own exclusive sovereignty. And yet as international trade expands, as inter-continental travel and communications become commonplace, as people move from one country to another, the interdependence of the human race is increasingly apparent. It is a tragic paradox that at such a time as this nationalism should be such a potent force, threatening the future of civilization itself by unleasing the weapons of mass destruction. This is the major political issue, dwarfing everything else we have discussed in the preceding chapters; for in the end the solution to every domestic problem depends on the wider context in which it is set. Unless we can establish peace and find ways of developing world co-operation across the boundaries of countries and continents, anything that we try to achieve within our restricted territorial domains is under threat. Hence the vital importance of strengthening the international agencies, such as the European Community, the Commonwealth and the organs of the United Nations.

What, then, are we to say about the nation-state, the exclusive self-interest of which is the obstacle to effective international co-operation? In his inaugural lecture on appointment to the chair of Politics at the University of Leeds, Professor David Beetham raised the provocative question whether the nation-state had now outlived whatever usefulness it once may have had. It is often forgotten that it is a comparatively recent development. As Beetham says, 'If we consider European history, then it is only the period from the seventeenth to nineteenth centuries that saw the definite emergence of the centralized *state*, successfully claiming a monopoly of law making and law-enforcing power, and a monopoly of political allegiance, over a unified geographical territory. Before that time political authority had been mainly local in its exercise, and subject to overlapping jurisdictions and multiple competences.'[1] He goes on to question whether it is any longer capable of dealing effectively with the economic, military and cultural problems which now confront us in our interconnected world.

This thesis is calculated to provoke a hostile, emotional reaction on the part of those who have come to take patriotism for granted as an obvious, if not over-riding virtue. Nobody would want to question the genuine values enshrined in it: devotion to home and family, to the land of one's birth, to the culture in which one has been brought up, to the people with whom one has been associated; and those are rightly honoured who have sacrificed their lives in defence of all this against aggression. But propaganda and muddled thinking can create an artificial ideal to which those undoubted values are easily prostituted. Without casting any reflection whatever on self-sacrifice for what are taken to be cherished ideals, we are bound to ask whether those ideals have been sufficiently clearly understood and whether they need rethinking in the light of changed circumstances.

When we are talking about the country to which we belong, what exactly do we have in mind? The territory bounded by seas, rivers, or lines drawn on a map? Or are we referring to people of a common race, language or culture? Or are we thinking of a set of shared values such as freedom and tolerance? Or again, is our notion of country defined by the political institutions to which we are subject? I suspect that very few people could answer these questions with any precision. The idea of nation or country is a confused amalgam of all these factors, felt rather than coherently related to one another. When they are examined, they almost all turn out to be ambiguous and incapable of satisfying the criteria of a defensible political entity.

This is most obvious when the boundaries of a nation-state are drawn geographically. For those, like ourselves, who live on an island surrounded by the seas, this may at first seem to be an obvious definition, but most peoples are not so situated. Sometimes rivers and mountain ranges provide convenient barriers of demarcation, but more often territorial boundaries have resulted from treaties agreed by warring factions, and the division is an arbitrary one, shown to be so whenever people move across them. Even the territory of an island, like Britain, does not settle the question of nationhood, as distinctions between Scots, Welsh, Irish and English make plain on the one hand and interchange with the European continent on the other. As long as people freely move across physical barriers, those barriers cannot define them unless they are artificially made to do so. As the world contracts through travel and communications, the territorial division of a nation makes less and less sense.

Identification by a common race, language or culture is a more promising criterion for the preservation of the nation state; for these do distinguish peoples from one another. However, the two super-powers are certainly multi-racial and multi-cultural, while different languages are preserved within them, more so in the Soviet Union than in the United States, though even there the various ethnic communities jealously guard their traditions. Every effort is made to persuade the American people that there is a distinctive way of life which binds them together, but in fact they are related to one another by many different ways of life, and by comparison with religion, culture and tradition the common bond is much more superficial, largely defined by geographical boundaries and the federal institutions of government. This is equally true of Canada. When I was living there, Prime Minister Diefenbaker frequently appeared on television with the opening sentence 'My fellow Canadians', but I always found myself wondering what chords he was actually touching, bearing in mind the totally different loyalties of English-speaking Ontario and French-speaking Quebec, not to mention the numerous immigrant communities of Dutch, Germans, Poles, Italians, Lithuanians,

Latvians and so on.

In Britain we are already a multi-cultural society. Before immigration from the West Indies and the Indian sub-continent, we were a mixed race derived from early European conquests and having developed distinctive strains in Scots, Welsh, Irish and English with a considerable Jewish community concentrated in certain districts. Those who try to put the clock back are fighting a hopeless rearguard action. Mobility makes for cultural interchange which may for a time weaken old ties, but the strength of cultural tradition persists, and there are many around prepared to do battle for its preservation and nurture. Variety adds immeasurably to the richness of life. Who, for example, would wish to see the death of the Welsh Eisteddfod or the Scottish Highland Games in the interests of a dull British uniformity? Nor is this phenomenon peculiar to Britain and North America. Every nation is experiencing cultural diversity, with migrant workers all over Europe and communal rivalries in every other part of the world. Cultural and linguistic associations can no longer be separated by national boundaries.

Christians have already begun to experience their membership of a world-wide family which transcends the frontiers of race, class, culture and nation, making them a potential threat to the supremacy of the nation state as well as a prophetic symbol of a universal human community. This has its origins in the proclamation of the kingdom of God, the interpretation of the crucifixion of Jesus as breaking down the barrier between Jews and Gentiles[2] – a crucial divide in the ancient Near East – and the vision of the seer who looked to the new Jerusalem into which the wealth and splendour of the nations would be brought.[3] Unhappily, the history of the Christian church has not fulfilled these expectations. It has been divided nationally and confessionally. Wars have been fought under the banners of Catholic and Protestant, and denominations have sprung up exhibiting at times bitter rivalries and intolerance towards one another. The record has been a far cry from the fulfilment of the prayer of Jesus that his disciples might be one that the world might believe in him.[4]

Nevertheless in recent years there has been a rediscovery of the unity of all Christians not only in the purpose of God, but in the sight of God. When St Paul heard that there were divisions in the church at Corinth with parties claiming allegiance to himself, to Apollos and to Peter, and others daring to assert that they were the only true Christians, he wrote to them asking the rhetorical question, 'Is Christ divided?'[5] It answers itself: those who put their faith in Christ are united in him whether they recognize it or not, whether they give expression to it or not. Division is a consequence of human sin, a failure to live in accordance with an authentic profession of faith. This was not a prescription for uniformity. It allowed for differences of sex, race, culture, and even for distinctiveness in theological convictions and forms of worship, as many have come to discover. Jews did not become Gentiles, nor Gentiles Jews. But there was a unity which transcended all differences, binding together those who called themselves Christians, belonging to one another because they belonged to Christ.

Many have found this hard to accept. There is a natural human propensity to suppose that only those who think as you do, who follow the practices with which you are familiar, who are identified by the same partisan labels, can possibly be your blood brothers and sisters. But that is what the church is all about: uniting believers in one family across all the artificial frontiers of nation, race, culture, sex, class and denomination, heralding the unity of all mankind in the loving purpose of God.

That has been the inspiration of the ecumenical movement of modern times. The word itself refers to the whole inhabited globe. While it is mostly used in a restricted ecclesiastical sense to denote the growing together of Christians of all confessional traditions across the world, it points beyond that to the ultimate unity of human kind. To those caught up in the conflicts of these days between races, super-powers, nation-states and classes, that may seem to be an idealistic dream. But it is already a reality for those who have experienced it. The World Council of Churches, established in 1948, now embraces all the major Christian confessions apart from the Roman Catholic Church, with which it has growing fraternal relations since the Second Vatican Council, and its membership is drawn from all six continents and just about every country under the sun. The pattern is repeated on a smaller scale in national and local Councils of Churches where those of different denominations are beginning to learn to share their resources, worshipping and working together for the advancement of the kingdom of God. The goal of Christian unity is not to settle for the lowest common denominator of belief, but to achieve the highest common factor by mutual understanding and shared experience. One of the most unfortunate misapprehensions of ecumenism is to suppose that it involves the surrender of inherited traditions and indifference to truth. Far from it. Christians have begun to learn as they have come to know one another in depth how they may be enriched by traditions other than their own. There is still a long way to go. The ecumenical movement is as yet in its infancy, and there are many Christians who stand aloof from it. But it is established and growing, a challenge to everything that divides people from one another and a sign of hope for a war-weary world.

I have no wish to minimize the faltering steps which have so far been taken nor to underrate the religious bigotry which still persists, fuelling the fires of communal violence. Northern Ireland is a tragic case in point, though it should not be forgotten that the leaders of the churches in Ulster have been in the vanguard of those seeking reconciliation. Ian Paisley may capture the headlines with his sectarian rhetoric, but many others who do not get the same publicity steadfastly work to change the climate of hostility. All the same, the intolerance of the past has brought a harvest of bitterness which it will take long to eradicate. In the words of the prophet Ezekiel, 'the fathers have eaten sour grapes and their children's teeth are set on edge'.[6] A terrible price is being paid for the sins of the past. Yet, when all the failures of divided Christendom have been acknowledged, 'we are,' as one of the pioneers of the ecumenical movement once said, 'in the early years of universal Christianity'.[7] Those words were written nearly fifity years ago, and over the intervening period great advances have been made. Today a dream has become a reality.

The immediate reaction to such a claim is almost bound to be scepticism in the light of the religious conflicts which appear to show no signs of abating in many parts of the world. It is all very well to talk about growth in Christian unity, but what about the way in which people still find themselves in hostile camps because of their religious allegiance? In particular, the rise of Islam with its militant factions is one of the major threats to peace, and the

Middle East has long been in turmoil through the armed struggles between Muslims, Jews and Christians. The tragedy of the Lebanon has merely been the focus of much wider conflict.

That cannot be gainsaid. Religion has been and is prostituted to nationalist and tribal ambitions, adding a fanatical impulse to political adventurism. But that is not the whole picture. Here we are concerned with the contribution that Christians can make to the healing of such divisions, rooted in a much more profound understanding of the purpose of God as revealed in Jesus Christ. If the way forward which Christians have discovered through the ecumenical movement is achieving a unity which transcends denominational differences, this has something to say about the relationship to one another of those who profess different religious faiths. A start has already been made, for example, in the work of the unit for dialogue with people of other faiths in the World Council of Churches. Again, a small, but significant breakthrough has been achieved at the Selly Oak Colleges in Birmingham with the establishment of a Centre for the Study of Christian-Muslim Relations, staffed by an equal number of Christians and Muslims. Here openness and respect have been achieved, mutual understanding has been allowed to grow, and a way forward charted for inter-religious dialogue. These, and other ventures like them, are only tentative first steps, but they do point in the direction which we have to follow if the human family is to learn not only to live in peace, but to discover a richer common life through shared experience and understanding.

Christians, then, have a loyalty which transcends the nation-state, calling it in question in so far as it claims supreme allegiance. Once this is realized, it is seen to challenge the absolutism of all political systems; for, if there is only one absolute loyalty to the God who revealed himself in Jesus Christ our Lord, then every other allegiance is relativized, whether it be to a theological formulation or to a political ideology. One of the most important testimonies which Christians are summoned to bear is opposition to the absolutizing of politics and with it the absolutizing of the nation-state. That calls in question the definition of the nation in terms of the absolute values which its particular political system is held to embody, challenging the sharp polarization which lies at the root of every major conflict in the modern world. The threat of war is its symptom, not its cause.

Therefore, as world citizens we have to resist the tendency of governments of all complexions to exaggerate the distinctiveness of their own political systems, their policies and programmes in the interests of preserving their own power and maintaining national identity. The most glaring example of this is to be seen in the war of words between the super-powers and their allies. Nobody can seriously question the differences that exist, but it is also clear that they are accentuated by the way in which governments behave. To portray the international scene as if it were a game of Cowboys and Indians, with all the good on one side and all the evil on the other, is not only to invite conflict but also to distort the real state of affairs. This has reached potentially disastrous proportions in the war of words between the Soviet Union and the United States. Each castigates the other as the enemy of civilization, painting the picture in stark colours of black and white. Neither is prepared to acknowledge anything of value in the other's political system nor to admit to any serious defects in its own. The suppression of freedom in countries under Marxist domination, the regimentation of society in the interests of the governing bureaucracy and the expansionist foreign policy backed by a massive build-up of arms are taken in the West, and in the United States in particular, to constitute an overwhelming case for portraying the Soviet Union as the villain of the piece. Looked at from the other side, the tables are reversed. The American government is viewed as dominated by financial and business interests, prepared under the guise of the defence of freedom to further the exploitation of the poor even to the point of sustaining tyrannous military regimes in Central and Latin America. Moreover, Marxists see the Western democracies as corrupted by the rat race for monetary gain, where anything becomes acceptable if it can be done for personal profit, and they fear the spread of this infection to undermine what they claim to be their own achievements in raising the standards of the mass of the population.

On both sides of the divide there is a gross over-simplification of the political issues occasioned by a frenetic determination to absolutize individual freedom on the one hand and corporate responsibility on the other. Both are ambiguous concepts, as we have seen in earlier discussions. Both can be faulted in the way they are translated into practice. I have no wish to minimize the defects in either system, but neither is as demonic and destructive of all human values as its opponents make it out to be.

Let us take the Soviet system first. Listening to some Western propagandists, one would suppose that all Soviet citizens had been crushed into slavish obedience to the rule of a tyrannous oligarchy by which they had been reduced to mere cyphers, tools of monstrous oppression, starved of any human dignity. And yet family life goes on, children are educated, the sick are cared for, leisure is enjoyed, sports flourish, the arts are given expression, and the churches grow in the number of their adherents. Certainly political dissidents are suppressed, the media are controlled, and there are severe restrictions on all forms of voluntary associations. Nobody in the West who has enjoyed freedom of speech and action would wish to live under such a system. But the point I am making is that Communist government is not as destructive of every human value and aspiration as its militant opponents pretend that it is.

On the other hand, the Western democracies are not the complete caricature Soviet propagandists make them out to be: populations in thraldom to greedy financiers, dragooned into extending their power over more and more of the world's surface, and threatening the Soviet peoples with subjugation. However, they, too, see features of Western society which they do not wish to see exported to their own country: the casinos and the amusement arcades, the sex shops, the license of the media, the ghettos of poverty. At the same time, Soviet spokesmen largely ignore the provisions of the Welfare State and the numerous co-operative associations for the common good.

The truth is that both types of society embody the ideals of freedom and corporate responsibility. The mixture is different and the interpretation is different; the defects of one are not the same as the defects of the other. Again let it be repeated that I am not minimizing the significance of the differences. What I am asserting is that governments on both sides exaggerate these at the expense of serious attempts to look for common ground and a larger measure of mutual understanding.

Turning from those who wield political power to the mass of the people they represent, the common ground becomes more obvious. The vast majority on both sides of the Iron Curtain have no inclination to embark on a great crusade to change the system of government under which others live. They long to live at peace with their neighbours; the thought of war is abhorrent; they want to be left to do their jobs, bring up their families, mix with their friends, tend their gardens and plots and pursue their hobbies. They have to be worked up to nationalistic fervour by playing on their fears of losing whatever they cherish. But the common bond is there, weakening the case for claiming that the nation-state is defined by the ideals it enshrines. It is largely the traditions of government and the vested interests of those who are elevated to political power which preserve the distinctiveness of nations, and, as the world becomes more and more inter-dependent, this looks more and more an artificial imposition on the human race.

But the nation-state is with us, and its preservation maintains the power of statesmen and politicians. With it the defence of the realm assumes over-riding importance. The fear of aggression dominates the foreign policy of every government, leading to the potentially disastrous escalation of the arms race and the threat of nuclear catastrophe. I leave aside for the moment the moral question about the legitimacy of the manufacture, stock-piling and the ultimate use of such weapons. The endless debate about this only becomes earthed when we face up to the political problems which sow the seeds of conflict and which, if superficially analyzed, distort the whole perspective.

Aggression springs from two causes: the desire of power-hungry politicians to extend their sphere of influence or fear of others doing so. It is necessary to be clear which of these predominates in a given situation. In the past, wars have been waged principally for the first of these reasons, the most recent being the Nazi attempt at world domination and the Iranian crusade in the Middle East. While such expansionist ambitions are still prevalent elsewhere, it is doubtful whether they are any longer predominant. Fear of aggression has to a considerable extent taken their place in the perilous world in which we are living; and fear when sufficiently intense easily expresses itself in aggression; the animal that feels cornered and threatened fights back whether that feeling is justified or not. It is a much more dangerous and unpredictable disposition than naked ambition; for the latter can be calculated; the former cannot. The madness of a nuclear war is far more likely to break out through an explosion of fear than through a calculated plan of expansion. Any rulers contemplating deliberate aggression would have to assess the consequences and weigh the possibilities of success. Fear would be much more likely to lead to a pre-emptive strike without regard to any consequences.

The United States and the Soviet Union both portray each other as potential aggressors with expansionist aims at world domination. There is a measure of truth in both charges. The Soviet leaders would like to see Communist rule expanded to other parts of the world, not so much now, I believe, because of deeply-held Marxist convictions, but because it would do something to justify their own retention of power at a time when the system is under criticism in its own satellite countries and is not working out in the ways predicted in its own home lands. On the other side there are American business and financial interests which would like to extend their economic empire to other parts of the globe. However, it is more than doubtful whether either of the super-powers would contemplate going to war for either of these objectives. Both have had their fingers burned in military operations on a relatively small scale which have demonstrated the impracticability of establishing unchallenged power over peoples who are opposed to foreign occupation. The Soviet adventure in Afghanistan has become bogged down in the face of widespread guerilla resistance, and the experience, notably in Poland, of trying to hold proud peoples in subjection has shown how brittle this can be. Is it credible that the Kremlin would even contemplate extending the range of its problems in Europe in the light of the sort of resistance it would encounter even if it were militarily successful?

The Americans have had to learn a hard lesson in Vietnam which their current intervention in Central America simply underlines. And, as I write, pressures are mounting on Capitol Hill for the withdrawal of the marines from the Lebanon. What we are seeing is the increasing futility of military operations to secure political ends. Of course, there are the madmen around, some in high positions in the armed services on both sides of the Iron

Curtain, some in the leaders of terrorist organizations, and how to deal with them is the problem which now confronts us. But if one tries to take even a short-term view of the international scene, the prospect of deliberate military expansion, at least on a large scale, is receding.

What is not receding is the fear that aggression may take place, and it is this which has to be undermined if paranoia is not to reach proportions that lead to an explosion which nobody wants. Instead of conducting a propaganda war focussing on the supposed aggressive intentions of the super-powers and their allies, political wisdom dictates a sustained effort to understand the causes of fear on both sides and remove them. To rely on the nuclear deterrent as an instrument of international diplomacy is to escalate fear to the point at which nerves may crack and unimaginable destruction be unleashed. The balance of terror is an essentially unstable state. The relentless increase in the quantity and sophistication of armaments is serious enough; politicians do not seem to have grasped that the escalation of terror is still more potentially disastrous.

A start could be made to reducing mutual fear if there was a resolute determination to understand what lies behind it. For example, instead of concentrating on the phenomena of aggression – on the incursion into Afghanistan and the use of the mailed fist in Eastern Europe – which are the stock in trade of Western polemics, we should try to understand the genuine fears of the Russian people. After all, they did experience the invasion of the Nazi hordes and the slaughter of millions of their people, and, although the Europeans have no intention of repeating the crimes of Hitler and his henchmen, the Soviet leaders are not so certain given the behaviour of successive American administrations. The only occasion on which nuclear bombs were actually used was when American aircraft dropped them on Hiroshima and Nagasaki, and this has been followed by military intervention far from American shores: in Korea, Vietnam and the Middle East. Now the Soviets see similar adventures in the Caribbean and Central America; and with it all they feel themselves surrounded by hostile forces, poised to strike at the slightest sign of weakness.

The other side of the coin is the one with which we are familiar: the Soviet army dominating the countries of Eastern Europe which can be seen as defensive or aggressive according to the angle from which it is observed; and the same is true of Afghanistan. If I have concentrated on Soviet fears, that is because we need to begin to see things from another point of view if any progress is to be made towards genuine detente and allaying the fears which bedevil the international scene. The tragedy of the Reagan administration has been adopting anti-Communism as a moral crusade, and the NATO powers have been dragged along by the coat-tails. The propaganda war should be halted and put into reverse by taking steps to remove the most obvious causes of fear. A withdrawal from intervention in the Caribbean and Central America would be a notable advance. Neither Cuba, Nicaragua nor El Salvador is conceivably ever going to invade the United States. Marxist governments there may not be in the financial interests of American capitalists, but that is no excuse for military adventurism which brings the world to the brink of catastrophe. The peoples of these small countries should be left to work out their own destiny. Similarly, a Russian withdrawal from Afghanistan would go a long way to allaying the fears of the West.

So far I have said nothing about arms control or the nuclear threat. That is because the political problem takes precedence. It is hardly surprising that talks on the reduction of weapons make little progress and negotiations break down when mutual suspicions are left to fester and the fires of hostility are fuelled by the propaganda war. To work for disarmament under these conditions is like treating the symptoms without combatting the disease. Failure to get to grips constructively with the political issues has led the super-powers and their allies into an impossible impasse, particularly in regard to nuclear weapons. So intractable is the impasse that straight thinking and clear speaking have been abandoned, because the facts have to be camouflaged to make them tolerable to contemplate. Two examples of this will suffice. Government ministers persist in talking about defence, but the use of nuclear weapons will defend nothing. Once they were unleashed, they would destroy everything that makes life worth living, even if human life were to continue; and that is now known to be a dubious possibility for the millions who would be the recipients of retaliatory bombardment. Secondly, the use of the word 'defence' is made palatable by a manifest contradiction. We are told that the purpose of stock-piling the nuclear arsenal is that it should never be used because the consequences of doing so are too catastrophic to contemplate; it is simply a deterrent. But for it to be a credible deterrent, there must be a resolve to use it, and the occasions on which a red alert has been sounded show that this is really intended. It is impossible to have it both ways. Either there is a readiness to use nuclear weapons or there is not. If there is, then the argument for defence falls to the ground. Mutual destruction is contemplated. In the meanwhile we live with this contradiction under the umbrella of deterrence which becomes an increasingly fragile protection from reality as the fears escalate.

Faced with this dilemma, what is to be done? More than enough has been written about the disastrous implications of global warfare, and we now need to concentrate on ways of avoiding it. Three broad options emerge. The first is to continue with the policy of deterrence indefinitely in the hope that sheer terror will compel the adversaries to reduce their stock-pile of armaments. But, as I have already argued, fear begets fear, and this is a prescription not only for failure, but for disaster. There are some politicians in high places, though they are probably a very small minority, who do not recognize this, and one of our most immediate perils is that we shall find that this has been tacitly accepted because of the difficulty of any constructive negotiations. A kind of fatalism tends to weaken the resolve of those who see that changes in political attitudes are necessary if progress is to be made, and the unimaginative hawks then get their way.

The second option is to seek to change the political climate by constructive diplomacy, and alongside this patiently work for a reduction in armaments without immediately abandoning the ultimate deterrent. Within this option there is a range of alternative proposals: commitment to no first strike, a nuclear freeze, the scrapping of Trident and the removal of the threat of Cruise and Pershing missiles from European soil.

The third is unilateral nuclear disarmament: the conviction that these weapons of mass destruction are so immoral and so potentially destructive of civilization that any state of affairs is preferable to their manufacture, deployment or use. Those who hold this view, and millions do so, believe that diplomatic negotiations towards multi-lateral renunciation inevitably proceed too slowly to prevent a catastrophe, and that as long as a country possesses these weapons it may be provoked to use them as well as being open to a retaliatory strike.

The growth of the movement in favour of this third option has alarmed many Western statesmen and has led to a propaganda campaign to present it as naive, irresponsible and even treacherous. This is unjustified. Whereas there are doubtless many unilateralists who have not weighed the consequences and whose reaction to the horror of nuclear weapons is an emotional one, there are many others who have fully counted the cost and deliberately embraced the risks, still convinced that the direct consequences would be preferable to a holocaust. One such is Professor H. D. Lewis, one of the most distinguished living philosophers, who in a recent article has presented the possible consequences of unilateral nuclear disarmament in the blackest terms I have seen, and yet opts for this alternative to the continuance of the policy of deterrence. He pictures Western Europe under a monstrous tyranny, the coming of a new dark age, and the subjugation, if not extinction of people like himself. And yet he finds such martyrdom preferable to the scenario painted by those who anticipate the results of a holocaust. The reality of the former in his view is more acceptable than the possibility of the latter.[8]

For reasons I have already given, I believe that Lewis's scenario is greatly exaggerated. The Communist régime at its worst hardly measures up to the prospect he envisages. For some people, perhaps for independent thinkers like himself, the consequences could be tragic; there might well be a multiplication of Sakharovs. For the majority, life would go on with certain freedoms curtailed, but at least there would be hope of change and the crumbling of the system from within once the fear of external aggression had been removed. Moreover, those who paint the picture in the blackest colours underestimate the effectiveness of internal resistance which would undoubtedly follow any attempt to impose a Communist system of government on a hostile population. The experience of the Soviets in Poland would be repeated on a massive scale and before long the cracks would become huge fissures. As I have said, I doubt very much whether the Soviet government would contemplate an invasion of Western Europe even if they had overwhelming military strength and were convinced that they themselves would not be devastated. That is a matter of political judgment. But, if I am wrong, the alternative is infinitely preferable to nuclear war. Do those who contemplate the possibility of using these weapons for any reason whatsoever really believe that this would be justified in order to avoid the extension of what has happened in Poland, Hungary, Czechoslovakia and Eastern Germany? To say that this would be using a sledge-hammer to crack a nut is simply a way of pleading for some sense of proportion.

That is why I find myself a nuclear unilateralist. I do not believe that there are any conceivable circumstances which would justify the use of these weapons, and I have become convinced that their continued manufacture and stock-piling are too dangerous if any progress is to be made towards detente. But this stance is only likely to win a wider consensus of agreement if there is a change in political perceptions. It is to this that we should be bending all our energies: from the Christian standpoint of world-citizenship seeking to extend the range of mutual understanding while strengthening the agencies which provide the means of international co-operation.

The tragedy of the arms race is that it prevents the nations who possess the technological resources from devoting them to the problems of world poverty, hunger and disease. Almost three-quarters of all scientific research is tied in some way to defence contracts. The spokesmen of the nations of the Third World complain that the West has failed to grasp that from their point of view the problems they face are a greater threat to civilization than the prospect of a nuclear conflict. That may be to underestimate the consequences for their own people of the outbreak of war between the super-powers, but it does bring into focus not only the deterioration of the plight of millions of people, but the fact that they are even now dying of starvation and disease. What they are saying is virtually this: 'While you are preoccupied with preserving your political institutions and your way of life, our people have no life at all.'

The famous Brandt report presented the international case for grappling immediately with the scale of the problem, and proposed concerete measures for beginning to deal with it. As far as government circles are concerned, it has largely fallen on deaf ears. Instead of positive steps being taken towards implementing its wide-ranging proposals, overseas aid budgets have been cut and some people in positions of influence have argued that existing programmes should be drastically reviewed, with a view not to their improvement, but their elimination, the preposterous thesis being advanced that Third World countries have their economic future in their own hands. How can that be when they are exploited by Western business interests, subjected to trade discrimination and starved of appropriate technology to meet the particular requirements of their huge populations? Certainly their future must be directed by their own governments. Aid must not be administered as massive hand-outs: a resurrection on the grand scale of the Lady Bountiful. Condescending largesse is one thing; international co-operation in improving the terms of trade, financial investment and technical expertise to secure economic growth appropriate to the countries concerned are another. Of course there are problems. Corruption and inefficiency in Third World administrations can divert aid into the wrong channels, but that is one of the obstacles which has to be overcome. If the Western powers and the Soviet Union were to drop their propaganda war and collaborate together with all the resources at their command in raising the standard of living of the world's poorest people, enormous advances could be made. But the political leaders at present seem unable to lift their sights above the squabbles of the nursery. 'You hit me first. No, you hit me. You're a mean beast. I hate you.' That, frankly, seems the level at which East-West propaganda has for too long been conducted. Ordinary people all over the world have the right to demand that the infantile game should stop, and energies be redirected to solving the problems of the hungry, the sick and the destitute. Present priorities are clearly wrong, and at least we could make a start in the West towards reversing the trend by which the rich get richer and the poor poorer.

Nevertheless, there is a limit to human achievement, given even the maximum good will and the greatest wisdom of statesmanship. That limit is inexorably set by death: the death of the individual and the death of the human race. The last half of this statement may come as a shock because it is something most people have refused to contemplate. Even Christian apocalyptic, predicting the end of the world, has long been unfashionable and virtually excluded from the teaching of the church except amongst fringe minorities regarded as eccentric and not to be taken seriously. Yet it is an inescapable element in the biblical tradition, and one with which we have now got to come to terms. There have long been hints of this from the scientific community, with warnings that at some time in the far distant future the earth is likely to become uninhabitable through some natural cataclysm, but these have been ignored because the time-scale projected such possibilities into so remote a future that for untold generations it would not appear on the imaginative horizon. Within the space of a few years the discovery of nuclear fission has suddenly brought the prospect of imminent apocalyptic on to the threshold of our own life-time. It was not a wild religious fanatic who speculated on the statistical improbability of the human race surviving into the twenty-first century, but a Fellow of the Royal Society, the deputy chief scientific officer at the Royal Aircraft Establishment in Farnborough.[9] That was over ten years ago, but the radical changes in policy with regard to the control of armaments and the redirection of technology which Desmond King-Hele warned were imperative if the human race was to survive have not occurred. If anything, the danger has increased.

There will be those who will argue that King-Hele's book was too pessimistic. So it may have been. Indeed, the author could not bring himself to believe that statesmen and politicians would be so stupid as not to reverse the trend before it is too late. It is not inconceivable that human life will continue for generations to come if wisdom prevails. But we cannot be certain. Even then there is an end to all things as far as this world is concerned.

It is a strange quirk of human nature that we find this almost impossible to contemplate. And yet we all know that our own death is inevitable. The end of the world occurs for countless individuals every day. It comes too quite suddenly to large numbers of others in groups, when an aircraft crashes with the loss of everyone on board, or when over two hundred marines are obliterated by an explosion in Beirut. Why should the total extinction of the human race be thought to be different? By a trick of the mind we escape from the reality of our own death by projecting a future into the lives of our children, but they too will die. To say this is not morbid. It is simply facing inescapable facts. Death puts an end to all human achievement.

I believe that this is an intractable problem for the humanist. The only way in which he can make sense of the political struggle is to ignore the fact of death; for if man's destiny is in his own hands alone, then every achievement is doomed to ultimate extinction; the fact that it may last for a while may afford some temporary satisfaction, but the long prospect is devoid of hope.

By contrast, Christian apocalyptic provides a context within which politics begins to make sense. The word does not simply mean the end of the human struggle, but the unveiling of a new future: the gift of God in his graciousness as he comes to meet us in the experience of death. Resurrection through death is at the heart of the Christian faith. Instead of death being regarded as the final tragedy, the end of every human expectation, it becomes the gateway to eternal life, the fulfilment of our destiny. We are made for death that we may have life. Sometimes it comes as the gentle and kindly visitor, to use the words of St Francis of Assisi, as physical weakness brings the earthly story to its close; sometimes it comes after protracted pain and suffering; sometimes violently. But, however it comes, it is the Christian testimony that the Lord who passed that way himself through the agony of the crucifixion accompanies us in the transition. Numerous biblical passages bear testimony to this. 'Though I walk through the valley of the shadow of death, I will fear no evil: for thou art with me.' 'When thou passest through the waters, I will be with thee.' 'Lo, I am with you always, even unto the end of the world.' 'O death, where is thy sting? O grave, where is thy victory? . . . thanks be to God which giveth us the victory through our Lord Jesus Christ.'[10]

Therefore, I find it astonishing that anyone should suggest that the threat of a nuclear holocaust or the end of civilization requires a complete rethinking of Christian theology on the grounds that hitherto we have been able to assume a secure natural environment.[11] In so far as we have done so, we have managed to ignore the apocalyptic emphasis in the biblical tradition. But it has always been there and ultimately central to the Christian hope. The inescapable end has always been in the hands of God, whether we are thinking of the individual or the race. What is new in the nuclear age is that human beings may now have the capability not only of causing the death of large numbers of people, but of everybody. It is a distinction of scale, not of kind. Death is death, however it occurs and on whatever scale.

Nevertheless, it is clear from the Christian standpoint that we have no right to take it into our own hands, whether by suicide, murder or mass extermination. Death, I repeat, is intended to be in the hands of God, the apocalypse or unveiling of his mercy. Brought about by human agency, there is nothing further that we can do to redeem it. Man has shot his last bolt and the issue lies with God. This is the inescapable context within which all human aspirations and achievements have to find their meaning and fulfilment.

The significance for politics should now be obvious. Either it is a futile exercise, a desperate attempt to snatch a transitory *modus vivendi* in a meaningless existence, or it is the ordering of society in a pilgrimage to an eternal destiny. If it is the latter, then nothing of ultimate value is irrevocably lost. The fact that our institutions are temporary does not detract from their significance. We would not tell a child to stop building sand castles on the beach because the tide would wash them away. The value they have lies in the activity, in the creativeness, the healthy exercise and the fun. It is part of a child's development. So with all our human endeavours. They are not to be measured by what they achieve, but by the development of human potentiality and the quality of relationships resulting from them.

The Christian vision, therefore, provides both a context and an inspiration for political action. It does so whether there is a long road ahead for the human race or whether the end of the earthly story is near at hand. We do not know what the future holds, except that it lies in the merciful providence of God. That, and that alone, is our hope and security in this uncertain world. It was powerfully summarized by Bishop Bergraav, the Primate of Norway during the Nazi occupation, in a sermon preached at St Margaret's, Westminster, on the conclusion of hostilities. 'I was being shown the damage to London the other day by one of your leading politicians. "Isn't it terrible," he said, "that we've discovered that one bomb could now destroy the whole of the capital?" To which I replied, "Yes, my friend, but we also know that, if that were to happen, the city of God remaineth."'

In vain the surges angry shock;
In vain the drifting sands.
Unharmed upon the eternal rock
The eternal city stands.

NOTES

NOTES

Introduction

1. Lesslie Newbigin, *The Other Side of 1984*, British Council of Churches 1983.
2. Alasdair MacIntyre, *After Virtue*, Duckworth 1981.
3. E. R. Norman, *Christianity and the World Order*, Oxford University Press 1979.
4. Digby Anderson (ed.), *The Kindness That Kills*, SPCK 1984.

Chapter 1 Why Politics?

1. J. Enoch Powell, Review of Peter Hinchliff, *Holiness and Politics*, Darton, Longman and Todd 1982, in *Theology*, November 1982, pp. 475f.
2. Colossians 1.20.
3. Cf. Ephesians 2.11–16.
4. I Corinthians 10.11.
5. I Corinthians 12.14–18, 26–27 (New English Bible = NEB).
6. Mark 12.17.
7. Romans 13.1f.; cf. Titus 3.1; I Peter 2.13–17.
8. Athanasius, *Hist. Arian.*, 44.
9. Hinchliff, op. cit., p. 5.
10. Mark 11.27–33; Matt. 12.23–27; Luke 20.1–8.
11. Quoted by Cyril Garbett, *Church and State in England*, Hodder and Stoughton 1950, p. 17.
12. Augustine, *The City of God*, Bk 1, Preface, ET in Fathers of the Church, New York 1950, by Demetrius B. Zema and Gerald G. Walsh.
13. Ibid., II, 21.
14. Ibid., XIX, 21, but cf. XIX, 24, where Augustine is prepared to allow that a 'people' may be defined as 'a multitude of reasonable beings voluntarily associated in the pursuit of common interests', and makes the Roman people a 'people' and their weal a 'commonwealth' or 'republic'.
15. Ibid., V, 17.
16. Ibid., XI, 1.
17. Ibid., XIX, 17.
18. Ibid., XIX, 15.
19. Ibid., XIX, 5–7.
20. Ibid., XIX, 13.
21. Augustine, *Ep.* 138, ET in Fathers of the Church, New York 1953, by

Parsons, p. 48. Cf. *De Civitate Dei*, V, 24 and XIX, 17, where he says that 'the heavenly city, so long as it is wayfaring on earth, not only makes use of earthly peace but fosters and actively pursues along with other human beings a common platform in regard to all that concerns our purely human life and does not interfere with faith and worship'.

22. Cf. Karl Barth, *Church Dogmatics* II/1, T. & T. Clark 1957, pp. 172–8.

23. *Theology*, September 1981, p. 339.

24. W. Temple, *Christianity and the Social Order*, Penguin Books 1942.

25. Luke 4.18f.

26. Nathaniel Micklem, *What is the Faith?*, Hodder and Stoughton 1936, p. 201.

27. J. H. Oldham and W. A. Visser t'Hooft (eds.), *The Church and its Function in Society*, Allen and Unwin 1937, p. 210.

28. R. H. Preston, *Explorations in Theology* 9, SCM Press 1981, p. 38.

29. Robin Gill, *Prophecy and Praxis*, Marshall, Morgan and Scott 1981.

Chapter 2 Democracy and Participation

1. Frederick Copleston, *A History of Philosophy*, Vol. 1, Burns Oates 1947, p. 233.

2. A. D. Lindsay, *The Essentials of Democracy*, Oxford University Press 1929.

3. Max Beloff and Gillian Peele, *The Government of the United Kingdom: Political Authority in a Changing Society*, Weidenfeld and Nicolson 1980, pp. 38f.

4. Gerald and Patricia Mische, *Toward a Human World Order*, Paulist Press, New York 1977.

Chapter 3 Party Games and the Establishment

1. Peter Selby, 'The Spirituality of Monetarism', *Audenshaw Papers* 80, June 1981.

2. Jeremy Seabrook, *What Went Wrong*, Gollancz 1978, pp. 95f.

3. Ibid., p. 72.

4. Cf. Frank Welsh, *The Profit of the State: Nationalized Industries and Public Enterprises*, Maurice Temple Smith 1982, pp. 163ff.

Chapter 4 Freedom and Equality

1. T. H. Green, quoted by Ian Bradley in *The Optimists*, Faber 1980, p. 217.

2. Basil Mitchell, *Law, Morality and Religion in a Secular Society*, Oxford University Press 1967.

Chapter 5 A Humane Economy

1. Matthew 19.23 (NEB).

Chapter 6 Education for Living

1. Lesley Gow and Andrew McPherson (eds.), *Tell them from Me*, Aberdeen University Press 1980; Roger White and David Brockington (eds.), *Tales out of School*, Routledge and Kegan Paul 1983.

2. Arthur Hearnden, *Red Robert: A Life of Robert Birley*, Hamish Hamilton 1984, p. 142.

3. James Brabazon, *Dorothy L. Sayers: The Life of a Courageous Woman*, Gollancz 1981, p. 282.

Chapter 7 A Caring Community

1. Cf. Ian Bradley, *Themes and Personalities of Victorian Liberalism*, Faber 1980, p. 45.

2. William Beveridge, *Power and Influence*, Hodder and Stoughton 1953, p. 9.

3. Philip Beveridge Mair, *Shared Experience*, Ascent Books 1982, pp. 124f.

4. William Beveridge, *The Pillars of Society*, Allen and Unwin 1948, p. 420.

5. William Beveridge, *Voluntary Action*, Allen and Unwin 1948, p. 322.

6. Charles McKean, 'Why the Home Front is Collapsing', *The Times*, 15 December 1983.

Chapter 8 The Wider Context

1. D. Beetham, 'The End of the Nation State?', *The University of Leeds Review*, 1983, pp. 2f.

2. Ephesians 2.14.

3. Revelation 21.26.

4. John 17.21.

5. I Corinthians 1.12.

6. Ezekiel 18.2.

7. William Paton, *World Community*, SCM Press 1938, p. 75.

8. H. D. Lewis, 'The Sword of Damocles', *Theology*, January 1984, pp. 3–6.

9. Desmond King-Hele, *The End of the Twentieth Century*, Macmillian 1970.

10. Psalm 23.4; Isa. 43.2; Matthew 28.20; I Corinthians 15.55–57.

11. Cf. Peter Selby, 'Apocalyptic – Christian and Nuclear', *The Modern Churchman* XXVI, 2, pp. 3–10.

INDEX

INDEX